PT ☆ 109

*I cried like a baby all day when I heard he'd died.
You can't know how special he was to all of us. I felt
that day like I'd lost the best friend of my life. That's
what John Kennedy meant to me.*

—GERARD ZINSER, Motor Machinist's Mate, PT 109

*Lieutenant Kennedy was one hell of a man. . . .
I didn't pick him for my skipper, but I kept thanking
God that the Navy had picked him for me.*

—BILL JOHNSTON, Engineer, PT 109

PT ☆ 109

John F. Kennedy
in World War II

ROBERT J. DONOVAN

with a new foreword by Daniel Schorr

McGraw-Hill

New York • Chicago • San Francisco
Lisbon • London • Madrid • Mexico City • Milan • New Delhi
San Juan • Seoul • Singapore • Sydney • Toronto

McGraw-Hill

A Division of The McGraw-Hill Companies

Copyright © 1961, 2001 by Robert J. Donovan

Foreword to the 40th Anniversary Edition by Daniel Schorr
Copyright © 2001 by The McGraw-Hill Companies, Inc.

Afterword to the 40th Anniversary Edition by Duane Hove
Copyright © 2001 by The McGraw-Hill Companies, Inc.

Portions of the Preface to the 40th Anniversary Edition are revised
and abridged from *Boxing the Kangaroo: A Reporter's Memoir*
by Robert J. Donovan, by permission of the University of Missouri Press.
Copyright © 2000 by the Curators of the University of Missouri.

A portion of the proceeds from the sale of this book is donated to the
John F. Kennedy Library Foundation.

Library of Congress Cataloging-in-Publication data is available.

2 4 6 8 10 DOC 9 7 5 3 1

Text design by Dennis Anderson

ISBN: 978-0-07140-868-4

To Marth

FOREWORD
TO THE 40TH ANNIVERSARY EDITION

DANIEL SCHORR

WHATEVER HAPPENED to the willingness of those who would aspire to be the nation's leaders to face personal risk in service to that nation? Is the willingness always there, latent, waiting only for circumstance to call it forth?

Since the late 1980s the mantle of America's leadership has passed from a generation that came of age in World War II to one whose concepts of military service were shaped in the murky moral and political minefields of the Vietnam War. The reissuance of *PT 109* comes at a propitious time to underscore the significance of that generational change and its impact on political discourse.

What Lieutenant John F. Kennedy did in the Solomon Islands was extraordinary. His motor torpedo boat rammed by a Japanese destroyer, he dived overboard and spent thirty of the next thirty-six hours in the water to rescue his crew. Ten weeks later, in command of another PT boat after refusing an offer to return to the States, he rescued a stranded Marine patrol under enemy fire. But, to Kennedy, to be fighting in a cause generally understood and supported was ordinary. He was only one of seven future presidents who volunteered to serve.

There was, of course, General Dwight D. Eisenhower.

Then Lyndon B. Johnson, naval reservist, the first member of

Congress to volunteer on the day after the attack on Pearl Harbor. He was in a patrol boat crippled by Japanese fire.

Richard M. Nixon, a young lawyer, served in the Pacific as a Navy lieutenant in the Combat Air Transport Command.

Gerald Ford joined the Navy as an ensign and served aboard the aircraft carrier U.S.S. *Monterey* in combat in the Pacific.

Ronald Reagan, Army Air Corps reserve officer, was barred from overseas service because of poor eyesight and, instead, made training films.

George H. W. Bush, Navy pilot, was shot down on a mission to bomb a Japanese-held island and rescued by a submarine.

There were many other future politicians who willingly served in World War II and did not make it to the White House. Robert Dole lost the use of an arm serving with the U.S. Army in Italy. George McGovern flew 35 combat missions as a B-24 bomber pilot operating from Italy. Lloyd Bentsen was also a bomber pilot stationed in Italy.

Sergeant Daniel Inouye served as a patrol leader with the Fifth Army's "Go-for-Broke" regiment in Italy; he advanced alone against a German machine gun nest, and his arm was shattered by a rifle grenade. Barry Goldwater served as a pilot in the Army Air Corps and came home a captain with a chestful of medals, including the Distinguished Service Cross.

There were not hawks and doves then. There was no soul-searching about whether this was a just war. The Axis drive for conquest, the declaration of war by Germany and Japan, left little to be discussed other than how it had come about. In discussions with his PT 109 shipmates, Kennedy talked about the timidity and apathy that had paralyzed the democracies in the 1930s.

In contrast, the future politicians of the Vietnam War generation reached arms-bearing age to confront a war without consensus and without the galvanizing impulse of a clear and present danger. They heard no clarion call—only conflicting, ambivalent messages of duty, framed in opposite terms by hawks and doves. Lacking an absolute imperative, they responded in relative terms.

Former Vice President Dan Quayle joined the Indiana National Guard in 1969, and during his six years as a National Guardsman went to law school and worked in the governor's office.

Former President Bill Clinton managed to avoid being drafted by a combination of deferments and ROTC assignments.

George W. Bush, who would be president eight years after his father, found his way into the National Guard. He spent the Vietnam War stateside and later said, "I'm very proud of my service."

Attorney General John Ashcroft received seven draft deferments for the seven years he was eligible for service.

Newt Gingrich, a great battler in Congress, did not serve in the military, nor did Senator Phil Gramm.

Other politicians did serve in Vietnam, Senators Bob Kerry and Chuck Robb notable among them. Senator John McCain endured years of imprisonment and torture as a POW in Hanoi. But Vietnam was not a generally supported war, and did not elicit the reflexes that sent a Jack Kennedy into battle. There are men prominent today who were born too late to answer World War II's compelling call. Their ambivalent responses to the Vietnam War mirrored America's deep divisions, which is why the contrast between John McCain and George W. Bush's military service was not enough to make McCain the Republican nominee for president in 2000.

We can suggest that if Bush, Clinton, and their contemporaries had come of age in 1942, they too would universally have answered the call to self-sacrifice. We can believe that still, today, there is in our nation's young men and women the innate love of country and spirit of self-sacrifice that wait only to crystallize around an absolute imperative. At the same time, though, we have to ask what the long absence of such imperatives has done to our nation's political discourse. You can perceive the generational change by comparing the Kennedy inaugural address on that frigid January 20, 1961, with the Bush address of forty years later.

Kennedy's speech was about sacrifice. He spoke of the graves around the world of young Americans who answered the call to service. He evoked the image of a "new generation of Americans, tempered by war, disciplined by a hard and bitter peace." And, the line most repeated, "Ask not what your country can do for you, ask what you can do for your country."

By contrast, the Bush inaugural speech seemed far from war or bitter peace. It was about more mundane values like "civic duty" and "compassion and character." Bush summoned Americans to be "responsible citizens" and to "serve your nation, beginning with your neighbor."

His address did not summon Americans to danger or to sacrifice. It was not only that the National Guard pilot speaks in a different cadence than the torpedo boat skipper. It is that the world has changed: America is not in danger, and asking what you can do for your country sounds a little quaint. If the political class of the Vietnam time talks more in terms of self-indulgence than hardship, perhaps it is because that is what their audience wants to hear.

World War II left this country with its head held high, celebrating a generation of heroes. The Vietnam War left this country with a divisive legacy and a less certain moral compass.

That is why it is such a good idea to read *PT 109* once again. This salutary book brings back the days when men heard an undeniable call to service in something bigger than themselves, and answered in kind.

DANIEL SCHORR is Senior News Analyst for National Public Radio. His half-century journalistic career has earned him, among other awards, three Emmys and the Alfred I. duPont–Columbia University Golden Baton for "Exceptional Contributions to Radio and Television Reporting and Commentary"—broadcasting's equivalent of the Pulitzer Prize. He is the last of Edward R. Murrow's legendary CBS team still fully active in journalism.

PREFACE
TO THE 40TH ANNIVERSARY EDITION

ROBERT J. DONOVAN

IF A LONG LIFE is its own reward, then a writer whose work survives with him is doubly blessed. It is a pleasure to write this preface for the fortieth anniversary edition of a book that has always occupied a place of honor in my memories. *PT 109* is a story from one tumultuous era of our nation's history that was written during another. Between January 1961, when I started researching the book, and its publication in November of the same year, our nation witnessed the Bay of Pigs invasion fiasco, a failed summit between Kennedy and Soviet premier Nikita Khrushchev, and the building of the Berlin Wall. Events that year would lead to the Cuban Missile Crisis in October 1962—and who can say to what extent Kennedy's experiences as skipper of a plywood naval patrol boat in 1943 prepared him for the qualities of leadership he exercised when the world moved to the brink of nuclear war?

At the approach of John F. Kennedy's inauguration as the thirty-fifth president of the United States in January 1961, I got a call from Ed Kuhn Jr., editor-in-chief of McGraw-Hill's trade book division, asking me if I would try my hand at a book about Kennedy's adventures as skipper of PT 109 in the South Pacific during the war against Japan. I liked Kuhn's idea. Working on such a book could bring me, the Washington bureau chief of a Republican newspaper (the *New York Herald Tribune*), a particular entrée to the new president. I told Kuhn I knew Kennedy. I had covered much of his 1960 campaign and was sure I could get his help on the book.

Unquestionably, Kennedy's reputation as a war hero had helped him win the election. After the war the author John Hersey had written an article entitled "Survival," which was published in the *New Yorker*. In the article, Hersey described how the boat commanded by Ambassador Joseph Kennedy's son had been wrecked in a collision with a Japanese destroyer and the young Kennedy had gallantly helped rescue most of his crew.

With inaugural festivities in Washington already swirling, I would have to wait until late January to talk to the new president. From my own experiences in the infantry, I knew that it was common for episodes to be recounted as being more exalted than they in fact were. Before undertaking a war book, ought I not satisfy myself that the subject was as it was hailed? Was there any unknown aspect of the ramming of PT 109 and the aftermath that, if disclosed, would shed a different light on the episode? Who could tell me? Who, for example, was certain to have heard through naval sources about any act or circumstances that had not come to light?

There was precisely such a person: Admiral Arleigh Burke, chief of naval operations and a member of the Joint Chiefs of Staff. In the war, ships under his command were in action the same night that Kennedy's boat was shipwrecked and in waters not far removed.

Admiral Burke had flourished in the Eisenhower administration, but rumors at the Pentagon had it that he was rather at odds with Kennedy. I made an appointment with Burke. In his office at the Pentagon I explained why I had to be circumspect in a book on PT 109. He understood me. He swung to the right in his chair and looked out the window. Then he swung back and said, "On that, Kennedy was all right."

A COUPLE OF DAYS after the 1961 inauguration, I was seated by President Kennedy's desk. Through Pierre Salinger, his press secretary, the president knew I was eager to write a book on his dramatic wartime experiences in the South Pacific.

"Oh, Bob," Kennedy said to me, "don't get into that. You'll be flogging a dead horse."

Referring to Hersey's article, he continued:

"Every time I ran for office after the war, we made a million copies of that article to throw around. There is really nothing more for you to tell."

I could not let that stand.

"If Ambassador Kennedy's son, the now-sitting president of the United States, was a naval officer whose boat was rammed by the Japanese in the war, leaving him shipwrecked in the South Seas," I said, "there would be a lot more to tell about it than can be covered in an article a few thousand words long. We are now at that point, Mr. President, where every phase of a president's career becomes the subject for a separate book. A book like this would be in libraries and archives. Future readers might never come upon the Hersey article in old magazines."

While I was still at the president's desk, Ted Reardon, a delightful member of Kennedy's staff, came into the room and overheard some of the conversation.

"Ted," the president interposed, "tell the navy to make anything they have on this subject available to Bob." Then he turned to me and said, "So go ahead and work on it, if that is what you want to do. If you still think you have a book, come back and I'll help you if I can."

I DEVOTED EVERY SATURDAY for the next couple of months to travel to interview surviving member of Kennedy's PT 109 crew. The men were scattered from Massachusetts to California, from Florida to Illinois. They were intelligent workingmen, mostly.

They regarded their disastrous collision with the Japanese destroyer *Amagiri*, and their subsequent rescue, as the most dramatic event of their lives. It was evident that they all admired, and in some cases revered, Kennedy for his skill and leadership in averting their capture and death at the hands of the Japanese. All told me essentially the same story with altogether a profusion of fresh detail.

While these interviews carried me a long way, they also left gaps. Different crew members, for example, remembered the sequence of events differently, which tortured narrative. None knew the names of the three islands, one after another, on which they found safety. On this score, the navy's maps were of no help.

I knew from the beginning that I would have to talk with the Australian coastwatcher who had helped arrange the rescue. It had also become clear that a very good war story could not be told adequately through interviews alone. I did not even have a clear picture of the scene, which sometime later I found described in these Robert Louis Stevenson lines:

Billows and breeze,
Mountains and seas,
Islands of rain and sun.

There were hundreds of islands in that region of the Solomons, and I had no choice but to visit some of them. Maps indicated that the area I needed to explore was twenty-four miles long and a minimum of five miles wide.

I was not looking forward to making my way alone among those distant tropical islands. Then I got word that the *Saturday Evening Post* had purchased the rights to publish five parts of the book. The magazine retained Elliot Erwitt of Magnum Photos to accompany me on my trip. He would fly from Paris to Los Angeles to join me. I soon found that he was a marvelous traveling companion and the finest photographer I ever knew.

We spent most of June in the Pacific, where a few lucky breaks and a lot of help and enthusiasm yielded better results than I could have dared hope. When I stepped onto the small beach at Plum Pudding Island, it seemed incredible that the man who was now president had once hidden in its heavy shrubbery with his crew to avoid discovery by Japanese scouts. For a souvenir for the president, I took a stick of coral from the adjacent reefs. When I saw him in the White House months afterward, he seemed especially delighted with it. I remember him walking along the corridor between the White House proper and the Oval Office, slapping the stick of coral against his thigh. It would have been hard for me to imagine that that piece of coral, shortened and bejeweled, would, some thirty-five years later, bring his widow's estate $68,500 at auction.

After interviewing the officers and crew of the *Amagiri*, I finally returned to Washington from Tokyo in July 1961, only to find that the *Saturday Evening Post* had decided to combine the final two parts of the book and run them in the Thanksgiving issue. They would have to have the entire manuscript on the day after Labor Day, which put me in a squeeze. My vacation at the *Herald Tribune* was ended. I had to get up at six every morning and write from 6:30 to 10:00 A.M., when I would leave for the office. The more I wrote, the more I was convinced that President Kennedy should read the manuscript. This was the opposite of my determination in 1956 that President Eisenhower should not see my book about him *(Eisenhower: The Inside Story)* before it was published. That was a political book about a president in office who might well feel pressures to request changes in the book. The Kennedy book was about a man's experiences in war. He was there; I was not. If I had made any mistakes in reporting eighteen years after the event, he would be in a position to correct me.

As the manuscript lengthened and the summer wore on,

Kennedy did not find the time to read the pages. Finally, Salinger told me that the president was going to the family compound on Cape Cod for a four-day rest. "If we can ever get him to read it," he said, "it will be there." I gave Salinger seventy-five pages to show Kennedy and waited until the following Tuesday for Kennedy to return. Still not a word. Then around 6:15 my phone rang in the office. A Secret Service man was calling from Hyannis Port, Massachusetts. "Mr. Donovan," he said, "Ambassador Kennedy would like to speak to you." Ambassador Kennedy?

"Bob!" came a pained voice. I knew Joseph P. Kennedy through my sister, who had been one of his secretaries in New York for a few years. "Bob," he wailed. "This is the worst book I have ever read! It's about my own son, and I'm bored to death with it." These words were the very first reaction I heard about the manuscript from anybody.

"What," he asked, "have you got all these islands in here for?"

"Where," I replied, "do you think the war was—"

"Why don't you write like Hersey?" Kennedy asked. "He's a good writer."

"Teddy didn't like it either," he added. As I was to learn, the former ambassador was wrong on this.

"But that business about PT 59," he ruminated, "will be duck soup for the movies."

"I don't give a damn about the movies," I retorted. "I'm interested in writing a good book, and—"

"Oh," he interjected, "you don't give a damn about the movies? Everyone in the country has money but the newspaper people, and you don't give a damn about the movies."

ULTIMATELY, JFK read the galley proofs. He corrected some dates in his schedule before going overseas. No change was made in my accounts of the actions at sea in which he was involved.

Not one of these accounts had come from him. They came from his crew, the islanders who rescued him, the Australian coast-watcher, and a variety of naval officers.

Obviously, the president did not object to a movie about himself, but he wanted his father, once a Hollywood mogul, to make sure any such movie did not wind up an embarrassment. He considered my book a fair representation of the facts. "The president had enjoyed the book," Salinger wrote in his memoir. "He particularly had been appreciative of the great amount of research done by Donovan, including a trip . . . to the South Pacific where he had found the natives who had rescued Kennedy and his crew, as well as the Australian coastwatcher who had played a key role in the affair." Thus, when Warner Brothers independently announced that it would, for the first time, make a movie—*PT* 109—about a president in office, Joseph Kennedy got Jack Warner to agree to base the movie on my book.

Kennedy also wanted a say in who would portray him in the movie.

With the terms agreed to, work on the movie went forward. The filming was done in the Florida Keys. Late in the fall, the executive producer, Bryan Foy (part of the old-time vaudeville act Eddie Foy and the Seven Little Foys), called to ask me to meet him in Miami to discuss some problems. When I joined him, he reminded me that the movie contract called for the president to approve the actor who would play the role of Lieutenant Kennedy. Foy asked me to talk to the president to get things moving. Kennedy was at Palm Beach. When I arrived the next afternoon, he was out on a yacht until four o'clock. I rented a bicycle and rode up along a public path to the dock. Landing in good spirits, the president came up to me and asked, "How's the book going?" "Oh, brother!" I said. "You deserve it," he replied. I told him why I was there and asked him if he had made up his mind on who should play the part of Lieutenant

Kennedy. As he often did when he was reaching for an answer, he tapped his right thumbnail against his front teeth.

After a pause, he said, "Jackie would like to see Warren Beatty play the part."

Shortly afterward, I called Foy in Miami, thinking he would be relieved at how fast I had obtained an answer. I did not sense that he was relieved at all, but I had done my part.

As it turned out, Foy had reason for skepticism. Beatty refused the part. "Beatty turned out to be an intelligent, sensitive young man," Salinger later wrote. "He told me there was nothing in the world he would rather do than play President Kennedy, whom he admired, but he saw no future in the picture in the hands of Bryan Foy."

Eventually, to settle the question of the leading actor, Warner sent to the White House some film clips of various actors. In the end, Kennedy and Salinger chose Cliff Robertson. He lacked Kennedy's sharpness, but on the whole he played his part well. Whatever the merits of the movie, it has attracted viewers on late-night television for the past forty years.

PT 109 was published in November 1961. During Thanksgiving weekend I received a call from President Kennedy, who was in Hyannis Port. He was elated by the success of the book and was very gracious about my work.

"What did your father think of it?" I inquired.

"Here, ask him," the president said, handing over the phone.

"Great book!" the former ambassador exclaimed. "See, Bob, you did just what I told you to do about pace. That brought it off."

I can vouch that the word *pace* had never passed between us. I did thank Mr. Kennedy, however, for persuading Jack Warner to base the movie on my book.

When the movie came out in 1962 the Kennedys invited me and my family to attend a showing in the White House. I had never met Mrs. Kennedy and was enchanted by her feathery voice. My two younger children, though, were more fascinated by little John F. Kennedy Jr.—"John-John." The president invited us to sit on the Truman Balcony with him while we awaited other guests. John-John came along with a box of toys and began heaving them over the high balcony without attracting his father's attention.

As usual, however, the Secret Service was on the job. Two agents stood on the lawn below to retrieve the toys and bring them back up in an elevator so that John-John could keep the air filled with projectiles.

There were no premonitions on that pleasant evening that the man who had escaped death under the most hazardous conditions in war would die in Dallas little more than a year later, victim of an assassin's bullet. I covered that story too, of course. Rereading this book now recalls Kennedy as I prefer to remember him, along with that epochal event—World War II—in which the seeds of his presidency were sown. What are the qualities of a good leader? I think the optimism and determination that marked his leadership of a few shipwrecked, wounded, and frightened men in 1943 served a great nation well in the darkest days of 1961 and '62.

Robert J. Donovan
April 2001

PREFACE

THIS BOOK is the product of 30,000 miles of travel to visit the places described here and to talk with many persons who participated in these events. I am deeply grateful to President John F. Kennedy and all the survivors of PT 109, whose recollections of their experiences in the South Pacific in World War II made this account possible. The President took the time to read it in manuscript and in galley proofs.

With Elliott Erwitt, the photographer, I explored all the islands on which the President and his shipwrecked crew were castaways in August 1943. I walked along the same reefs and swam in the same currents that they did.

To my astonishment all ten of the natives who in one way or another participated in the rescue of the President and his crew are still living in the Solomon Islands. For several days most of them accompanied us on our converted copra scow *Kingfisher* and showed us exactly what happened, how it happened and where it happened.

Part of the PT operations dugout on Lumberi Island, whence the President was sent on his fateful mission on August 1, 1943, is still standing. Japanese planes shot down by the PT boats in Rendova Harbor that afternoon still lie on the coral bottom where we could see them.

We first went to Sydney to interview Arthur Reginald Evans, the Australian coastwatcher who helped arrange the President's rescue. He generously gave me access to his log of messages dealing with the wreck of PT 109 and the rescue of the President and his crew. From Australia we flew to the Solomons to visit the islands that appear in this story, Rendova, Lumberi, New Georgia, Gizo, Naru, Olasana, Plum Pudding, Wana Wana, Gomu, Kolombangara, Leorava, Vella Lavella, Moli, and Choiseul.

Choiseul was the scene of an ambush of a large Marine patrol, in whose rescue the President played a dramatic part as skipper of PT 59, his second boat in the Pacific. As an epitaph to that engagement Mr. Erwitt and I found in the jungle a rusting Japanese helmet and a human skull imbedded in the sandy ground beside it.

From the Solomons we went to Tokyo where I interviewed about thirty officers and men of the *Amagiri*, the destroyer that sank PT 109 in Blackett Strait. These included the senior officer aboard, Captain Katsumori Yamashiro, former commander of the 11th Destroyer Flotilla, and Commander Kohei Hanami, the skipper. Because of the controversy as to whether the *Amagiri* rammed PT 109 accidentally or deliberately, I was eager to get the testimony of the man who actually had his hand on the wheel, Coxswain Kazuto Doi. He was ill at the time of my visit, but subsequently I obtained a written statement from him.

The Navy and Marine Corps gave me all extant reports bearing on this subject, some of which were declassified for the purpose. Accounts in this book about the disposition of PT boats in combat, including the position of the boats at the time 109 sank, are mainly based on official action reports.

On the background of episodes involving PT 109 and PT 59 no one was more patient and helpful than Captain Arthur H. Berndtson, a participant in the most memorable of them.

I received valuable assistance from others beside the survivors, who played roles of their own—Allen P. Calvert, Alvin

P. Cluster, Thomas G. Warfield, Commander Henry J. Brantingham, Robert Lee Rhoads, Jr., Pat Munroe, James A. Reed, John L. Iles, Paul G. Pennoyer, Jr., Lieutenant Governor Edward F. McLaughlin of Massachusetts, Deputy Attorney General Byron R. White, Richard E. Keresey, Lt. Col. Warner T. Bigger, Under Secretary of the Navy Paul B. Fay, Jr., P. A. Potter, William Cullen Battle, Charles F. Rowley, Jr., John Harllee, William F. Liebenow, James L. Woods, Captain Rollin E. Westholm, Bryant L. Larson, Carl S. Livingston, E. H. Kruse, Sidney Rabekoff, Joe G. Atkinson and Representative Torbert H. Macdonald among them.

In the islands, I was helped in particular by three men—John Leaney, a British Colonial Office official, Dick Harper, skipper of the *Kingfisher*, and Benjamin Kevu, one of the native scouts who speaks English and was my interpreter in the interviews with the other scouts.

In Japan Miss Haruko Hosono located members of the *Amagiri* crew for me and was a superb interpreter in my interviews. I was surprised to discover that Miss Hosono and her father are friends of the Kennedy family and had been the President's personal guests at the inauguration.

The facts about the strategic background of these actions come from Samuel Eliot Morison's *Breaking the Bismarcks Barrier* and *The Struggle for Guadalcanal*. Some of the biographical details of the President's early life are drawn from James McGregor Burn's *John Kennedy: A Political Profile*. Like everyone who writes on this subject I am indebted to John Hersey, whose article "Survivor" in *The New Yorker* in 1944 captured some of the dialogue still fresh in the memory of Mr. Kennedy and the crew.

Every detail of the book is accurate in so far as it was in my power to make it so. No scene was created out of whole cloth, no encounter fictionalized. The conversations are, of course, recreated but in roughly the words the participants remember using.

Finally, in the writing of this book I have had the tireless, imaginative and craftsmanlike help of Edward Kuhn, Jr., editor-in-chief of the Trade Division of the McGraw-Hill Book Company. And Mrs. Mary Moore Molony gave me skillful assistance in the research and editing.

Robert J. Donovan
Chevy Chase, Maryland
September 7 1961

THE WHITE HOUSE

September 20, 1961

Dear Bob:

I have read this book with great interest. I find it to be a highly accurate account of the events of the war. I have been particularly interested in the many facets of this story that you developed that I was not in a position to know at the time.

Sincerely,

John F. Kennedy

Mr. Robert Donovan
New York Herald Tribune
Washington, D.C.

Give me a fast ship for I intend to go in harm's way.

—JOHN PAUL JONES

ONE

ON APRIL 7, 1943, the United States Navy's LST 449 approached the northern coast of Guadalcanal. At 12:15 P.M. off Togoma Point the skipper, Lt. Carl S. Livingston, noticed several transports and destroyers racing out at high speed into Iron Bottom Sound, so named because so many ships had been sunk there before the Americans had finally wrested Guadalcanal from the Japanese.

At 12:20 P.M. the signal station at Koli Point flashed: "Condition Red." This meant that an air attack was imminent. Moments later a destroyer rushing by gave LST 449 a similar warning. Lt. Livingston ordered his ship turned about, and as quickly as he could he took out after the vessels fleeing through Lunga Roads.

LST 449 carried a heavy load of cargo and passengers, including a hundred and seventy Army replacements and a group of naval officers bound for assignments in the Solomon Islands. Among them was Lt. (jg) John Fitzgerald Kennedy of Boston, a bachelor a few years out of Choate and Harvard, who had recently completed the course at the Motor Torpedo Boat Squadron Training Center at Melville, Rhode Island. As a transient he had no duties aboard and was below in his bunk reading when Lt. Livingston began ducking from one destroyer screen to another for protection as the ships continued to clear the roads.

The sharp turns rolled Lt. Kennedy around in bed. He thought it strange, yet no word came from above to arouse concern. It could hardly have dawned on him or his fellow passengers that the Japanese had launched their greatest air attack since Pearl Harbor and that at this moment a hundred and seventy-seven enemy fighters and dive bombers were roaring toward Guadalcanal from Rabaul, New Britain.

Up on the bridge Lt. Livingston received orders to wait off Togoma Point for the destroyer *Aaron Ward*, now on the way to screen him, and LST 446, which was somewhere in the vicinity. In a few minutes he sighted the *Aaron Ward* racing toward him from the northwest, hull down, at full speed. LST 446 never did appear, but a unit consisting of the *Aaron Ward*, LST 449 and Sub Chaser 521 formed beyond Togoma Point and in full flight steamed toward Espiritu Santo in the New Hebrides.

Shortly before three o'clock sailors on LST 449 saw dots in the sky far to the east toward Cape Esperance, Guadalcanal. Gradually these dots grew into Japanese "Vals" and "Zekes," and soon many of them began peeling off to attack Henderson Field on Guadalcanal. To the north the men on LST 449 could see other planes swooping down on Tulagi, a small island off the coast of Florida Island north of Guadalcanal.

Lt. Livingston ordered his helmsman to start circling. He had good reason to. LST 449 was carrying, among other things, a cargo of bombs for the Russell Islands. A direct hit from the air might blow 449 and every man aboard into fragments. The circling motion of the ship was too much for Lt. Kennedy's curiosity. He climbed out of his bunk and made for the companionway.

Just about this time, at 3:10 P.M., a Japanese plane glided down out of the sun into the flaming guns of 449. Ten feet off the port bow a five-hundred-pound bomb splashed into the water.

A tremendous explosion knocked the ship into a 20-degree list to starboard and lifted the stern out of water.

Bound for the deck, Kennedy was nearly thrown off his feet. Above, a great fountain of water splashed across the ship. Moments earlier, Lt. Livingston had gone out on the port wing of the bridge near where the bomb fell. The explosion hurled him clear across to the starboard wing. He was soaked with salt water but did not immediately feel any severe pain, which was surprising because the concussion had fractured his neck.

Kennedy scrambled to the deck, and the sight before him remains to this day one of the most spectacular he has ever seen.

Nine enemy planes, some hurtling down in steep dives, others slanting in on long glides, were attacking 449 and the *Aaron Ward*. The bomb that blew Lt. Livingston across the bridge was followed by another that hit fifty feet off 449's port bow. Two more exploded off her starboard bow, and another spouted a geyser on the starboard side abreast of the bridge.

Kennedy was caught up in the frantic excitement on the deck. Each bomb landed close enough to drench the ship with water. Their blasts wrecked some of the landing boats, sprang bulkheads, demolished a pump and jarred a good part of the ship's mechanism out of order. Still, LST 449 avoided a direct hit. The *Aaron Ward* was not so fortunate.

While 449's gunners were firing furiously at a plane sweeping low across the horizon, they saw smoke rising from the destroyer. Rapidly the wisps grew into thick black billows, whose folds and creases glimmered with red flame. A bomb had torn the *Aaron Ward*'s engine room apart, and near-misses had flooded both firerooms.

As the destroyer began to settle in the water, LST 449 shook off the attacking planes and started for her side. However, before she could get there, a minesweeper moved in and took the *Aaron Ward* in tow. It was a game effort, but there was little hope. Three miles off Florida Island the *Aaron Ward* sank.

The chief quartermaster on board LST 449 reported to Lt. Livingston that two pilots had been seen parachuting into the sea from burning planes. One of them was in the water to the east of the ship, and since at least the first wave of the attack was over, Lt. Livingston went to his rescue. Kennedy turned his attention from the *Aaron Ward* and joined a group of soldiers and sailors who were hanging over the rail watching as 449 closed in on the flier.

Someone shouted a warning: the flier might resist capture. The ship's executive officer took a submachine gun and went out on the starboard wing of the bridge.

The Japanese drifted inert in his life jacket watching 449 approach until the bow crossed in front of him whereupon he yanked off his helmet, slipped out of his life jacket and began to swim away. Lt. Livingston gave orders to reverse the starboard engine. Kennedy and the others at the rail noticed that the man's stroke was peculiar in that he swam with his right hand under water all the time.

Finally LST 449 drew close enough for the lieutenant who was directing the rescue to throw a rope. Instead of taking it the Japanese jerked a revolver out of the water and fired two shots pointblank at the rescue party on the forecastle. Neither shot drew blood. Before he could pull the trigger again a torrent of bullets flew from small arms of all kinds. The burst of fire was annihilating. Lt. Kennedy saw the flier lift up both arms and collapse face forward into the sea.

"Welcome to the South Pacific," he said to himself.

LT. KENNEDY'S voyage had begun in San Francisco a month earlier, at 5:21 P.M. on March 6, when the U.S.S. *Rochambeau*, a Navy transport, sailed from Pier 34 bound for the New Hebrides a thousand miles northeast of Australia.

Her decks and portholes were blacked out as she glided

through the dusk under the Oakland–San Francisco Bridge and out the Bay past Alcatraz Island. The ship, then the well-appointed liner *Marshal Joffre* of the Compagnie des Messageries Maritimes, had escaped from Manila with a polyglot crew when the Japanese attacked the Philippines. After reaching Darwin, Australia, in the face of continuous peril, the *Marshal Joffre* sailed to the United States for conversion into a transport and was renamed the *Rochambeau*.

The ten-year-old vessel was now making regular runs between the West Coast and the South Pacific. On this particular trip she set out, after some last-minute generator trouble, with a group of transient Navy officers bound for combat assignments. She also carried orders to make a two-day stop at San Diego to take aboard fifteen hundred Navy enlisted personnel, after which she was to sail, mostly unescorted, out across the Equator to Espiritu Santo.

It would be quiet on the lower decks until the fifteen hundred sailors were packed aboard in San Diego. The main activity this first night out was on "A" Deck, where the transient officers were quartered in threes and fours. Most of them were young men heading for a combat zone for the first time from campuses and training centers. They wandered from stateroom to stateroom exchanging scuttlebutt and talking about their final leaves. At the start of the long trip many talked seriously about world affairs. They argued about men and events over which they could not have had the slightest control, but which were now exercising a fateful influence over their lives.

In the stateroom shared by Ensign James A. Reed and Ensign Paul G. Pennoyer, Jr., a debate waxed over Great Britain's prewar policies. Ensign Pennoyer had come out of Harvard to become a Navy torpedo-bomber pilot. He was J. P. Morgan's grandson. Ensign Reed, a product of Deerfield and Amherst, was looking forward to what seemed a most distant day when he would study law.

As neighboring officers drifted in and out, both Reed and Pennoyer took some notice of a tall, slim, polite stranger with a boyish shock of sandy hair, who had entered unobtrusively in a khaki shirt open at the throat and khaki pants cut well above the ankles. Unlike some other restless visitors, he lingered and listened. This was a night, however, when no one gave a damn about introductions, and neither Reed nor Pennoyer knew, or was particularly concerned, that his guest was Lt. John F. Kennedy.

Ensign Reed was devoting energies of mind and tongue to an arraignment of Neville Chamberlain and "appeasement." If Chamberlain had refused to compromise with Hitler at Munich, he argued, Germany would not have overrun Europe and so encouraged Japan to attack Pearl Harbor.

Kennedy spoke up. Why, he inquired, should all blame be placed on Chamberlain? The Prime Minister had gone to Munich in a fatally weak position. For this, Kennedy contended, a great many persons were responsible. There were too many shares of blame for one man to answer for all.

Ensign Reed replied that Munich was the critical moment. Chamberlain's capitulation to Hitler at that point ended the chances of stopping the tide of aggression.

If so, Kennedy said, blame the timidity and the apathy that had paralyzed the democracies in the 1930s. Blame the pathological dread of war and the pacifism that had softened Britain. Blame business and labor and political parties which had placed their own interests above rearmament. This was not a problem for Britain alone, but for all democracies and capitalist societies, Kennedy said.

Ensign Reed stuck to his point, but the thought crossed his mind that he was up against a good debater.

Kennedy was well schooled in his points. In his senior year at Harvard in 1939–40, when he was a candidate for a degree in political science, he had chosen "Appeasement at Munich" as the subject of his undergraduate thesis. The work was his chief scholastic effort that year. Under the supervision of Bruce Hopper and Payson Wild, professors of political science, he holed up in Widener Library, poring over the *Times* of London, the *Economist*, Foreign Office minutes and parliamentary debates.

His thesis followed the lines of his arguments with Ensign Reed. When he turned it in the reaction of the faculty was so favorable that he decided to try to get it published. His father, Joseph P. Kennedy, who was then Ambassador to the Court of St. James's, sent him some suggestions from London. Arthur Krock, of the *New York Times*, a friend of the Kennedy family, suggested calling the book *Why England Slept*. Another friend, Henry Luce, editor-in-chief of *Time*, agreed to write a foreword. Wilfred Funk, Inc., published the book in July 1940, and it soared onto the best-seller list. Reviews on the whole were favorable, and at the age of twenty-three its author became a person of considerable prominence in the United States and Britain. "You would be surprised," his father wrote from London, "how a book that really makes the grade with high-class people stands you in good stead for years to come."

This had been Kennedy's first serious academic effort and in the original form of the thesis it helped to earn him honors in political science. Previously he had not been known as a scholar at Harvard. In fact his average for his first two years there was only a little better than C. The head of Winthrop House where he lived, Professor Ronald Ferry, characterized Kennedy's Harvard career as "reasonably inconspicuous." Although he was a member of the editorial board of the *Crimson* for three years, he left no enduring mark there. In his early years athletics seemed more attractive to him than academic work. Although he weighed only 149 pounds when he was a freshman, he tried with a furious intensity to make the football, swimming and golf teams. While he succeeded in making the varsity swimming team, his athletic reputation was more for dedication than for ability. In any athletic contest he fought with the kind of fierce determination that left a lasting impression.

That night on board the *Rochambeau*, Kennedy argued with Ensign Reed and the others until two or three o'clock in the morning. Then, still without introductions, he said goodnight and returned to his own stateroom. The strong pulse of the ship, the tremble of the deck beneath his feet told him that they were now under full power, plowing ahead in the darkness. The brown hills of San Francisco were falling far behind, and it would be a long time before any of the passengers would see them again.

The next day Lt. Kennedy and Ensign Reed were introduced to each other and rapidly became close friends.† They stood at the rail on March 8 and watched as the *Rochambeau*, a diesel-powered vessel with odd-looking square stacks, pulled into the Broadway Pier at San Diego. They would have liked to go ashore, but this was not permitted. When the ship sailed two days later they stretched out on deck in rubber life belts, looking at a Navy blimp and a small patrol craft that were to escort them for the first forty-eight hours or so, after which they would be on their own for all but a small part of the trip.

Kennedy and Ensign Pennoyer also became friends. They shared a lively interest in the Middle East, which Kennedy had visited in 1939, and in a box of Roman Allones cigars, which someone had given Pennoyer before he sailed. One night after they had been at sea a week Pennoyer was standing at the rail of a dark deck when Kennedy came up to him and said he had some bad news. He had just seen the mimeographed news bulletins. J. P. Morgan, Pennoyer's grandfather, was dead of a stroke.

---

†Reed was an usher at the wedding of John F. Kennedy and Jacqueline Lee Bouvier in Newport, R.I., in 1953, and is now an official of the Kennedy administration.

As the *Rochambeau* pushed westward Kennedy used to read for hours at a time. The weather soon turned warm, and he and Reed would loll on the fantail in the sun discussing the books. Kennedy was particularly enthusiastic about *The Forty Days of Musa Dagh*, Franz Werfel's story of the stand of the Armenians against the Turks' campaign of annihilation in World War I. But more than any other book he read at the time, he said, he enjoyed *Pilgrim's Way*, the memoirs of Lord Tweedsmuir (John Buchan), British diplomat, scholar and author.

"I am going to send you a copy when we get back to the States," he promised Reed. The promise was kept.

As Reed discovered, Kennedy at twenty-five had already had an unusual life against an international background of wealth, political influence and diplomacy. Born on May 19, 1917, in a comfortable frame house in a lower-middle-class neighborhood in Brookline, a suburb of Boston, Kennedy had grown up in a large, good-looking and unbelievably energetic family, whose forebears had immigrated from Ireland and acquired political power in the Democratic Party in Massachusetts. His parents, Joseph and Rose Fitzgerald Kennedy, had been married by William Cardinal O'Connell and had nine children: Joseph, Jr., John, Rosemary, Kathleen, Eunice, Patricia, Jean, Robert and Edward, who were reared in the Catholic Church.

The elder Kennedy, having begun life in modest circumstances, graduated from Harvard and at the age of twenty-five became president of a small East Boston bank. After World War I he amassed a fortune in finance and motion pictures. Because he managed his affairs from New York, his family lived in Riverdale and Bronxville during young Jack's boyhood. Jack attended schools in both communities, spent a year at the Canterbury School, a Catholic institution in New Milford, Connecticut, and then went to Choate, in Wallingford, Connecticut, before entering Harvard.

His father's political influence by this time was considerable. He supported Franklin D. Roosevelt before the 1932 Democratic National Convention, and the new President made him first head of the Securities and Exchange Commission. Through his father Jack Kennedy became acquainted with many of the leading men and women of the day, among them Franklin and Eleanor Roosevelt, Churchill, Eden, Hull and Farley. He spent his winter vacations at the family's house at Palm Beach and his summers at still another house his father had bought at Hyannis Port, on Cape Cod.

He reminisced to Ensign Reed about his experiences in Washington when his father was in the Roosevelt Administration and about his visits to London later when his father became the American Ambassador. He talked about his rough-and-tumble boyhood rivalry with his elder brother, Joe, who was now a Navy bomber pilot, based in England. His family, he said, had high hopes for a political career for Joe.

The Kennedy family was at one and the same time closely knit and violently competitive. Joe—handsome, driving, gregarious—was the leader and was not always easy on Jack. It was only after Joe's graduation that Jack came into his own at Harvard. Joe would be the war hero, the politician, the world figure like his father. For some time Jack dwelt in his shadow. After graduation from Harvard and before the war gave him direction, the younger brother was uncertain about his future. Perhaps the law, perhaps business, perhaps a writing career? He considered Yale Law School but dropped the idea. He entered Stanford business school but left after six months to make an extended tour of South America. As for a political career—Kennedy had failed to survive even the primaries in an effort to become freshman class president at Harvard.

Youthful in appearance, poised, apparently easygoing yet reserved, this was the young man who lounged on the fantail of the *Rochambeau* talking with Ensign Reed and heading toward a strange experience that, some would say years later, was to change his destiny.

Every day at dawn and again at dusk general quarters was ordered. These were the hours of maximum hazard from submarines. The transient officers had no particular stations to go to. In the afternoons, however, Kennedy was invariably an eager spectator at the daily gunnery practice. Occasionally, he would play bridge with his friends, who now included Ensign Charles F. Rowley, Jr., another Harvard man turned torpedo-bomber pilot. One of these games wound up with Ensign Rowley taking out his checkbook and writing Lt. Kennedy a check on the Brookline Trust Company for forty dollars.

On board the Navy issued the transient officers complete combat gear, including sheath knives and .38-caliber Smith & Wesson revolvers. Kennedy and his friends found the bowie knives useful. They put up a board in a stateroom, pasted pieces of paper on it and then, at ten feet, threw the knives at the paper, seeing who could score the most bull's-eyes.

Several times unidentified ships on the horizon caused alarms aboard the *Rochambeau*, but all of them turned out to be friendly. Except for a brief shutdown of one of the engines for repairs, the trip passed uneventfully. In fact, for Kennedy and his companions it was rather pleasant. On March 26 the U.S.S. *Tracy*, an old four-stack destroyer converted into a minesweeper, picked up the *Rochambeau* at the approaches to the New Hebrides and on March 28 escorted her into the heavily mined beautiful harbor at Espiritu Santo.

At the rail Kennedy and Reed watched the wreckage of a sunken transport slip by. It was their first view of the destructiveness of the war in the Pacific. As the *Rochambeau* swung farther up the channel, they were thrilled by the sight of a large fleet riding at anchor around the carrier *Enterprise*. Spread before them was an exciting panorama of twenty-one destroyers, the American cruisers *Honolulu, San Diego, St. Louis* and *Nashville* and the Australian cruiser *Leander.*

Reed's orders directed him to continue aboard the *Rochambeau* to Nouméa on New Caledonia. Kennedy's orders were to disembark at Espiritu Santo and proceed to the Solomon Islands for assignment to motor torpedo boats, a saucy breed of craft officially known to the Navy, and sentimentally enshrined in the hearts of the people, as PT (patrol, torpedo) boats. The two friends shook hands and parted, with Reed promising to volunteer for PTs as soon as he reached Nouméa in hope that they could get together again before long.

When Kennedy went ashore he was assigned to another group of transient Navy officers and marched aboard LST 449, bound for Guadalcanal, where the Army replacements were to be landed, and then to Tulagi, destination of the transient Navy officers.

The first days out of Espiritu Santo passed without any calamities. Several air alerts were sounded, but in those tense months everything that flew was presumed to be a Japanese plane, and men were whisked off to general quarters when the only aircraft in the area were friendly.

In spite of these alarms the thirty-seven-year-old skipper, Lt. Livingston, a native of Henderson, Kentucky, found time occasionally for quiet conversation over the green-covered table in his quarters. Early in the voyage he heard that one of the Navy passengers was the son of Ambassador Kennedy. Eager for a first-hand report on Europe before the war, Lt. Livingston sent for Kennedy.

"You must have seen a good bit," he ventured.

Kennedy replied that in his junior year at Harvard he had obtained permission to spend the second semester abroad. He told Lt. Livingston about his arrival in Europe in 1939 as the Nazis were about to swallow the remains of Czechoslovakia.

He recalled his tour of France, Poland, Russia, Turkey and Palestine. From the capitals he used to send his father in London his own appraisals of the situation in these countries.

Just before sailing for home at the start of his fall term, he recalled, he had returned to the British Isles in time to hear the portentous news of the torpedoing of the *Athenia* by a German submarine. He ended his story by recounting to Lt. Livingston how Ambassador Kennedy had sent him to Glasgow to assist American survivors who were brought to Scotland.

After the great air raid and the shooting of the Japanese airman on April 7, LST 449 and Sub Chaser 521 retired toward Espiritu Santo because it was feared that the Japanese might strike again in even greater force the next day. No enemy planes returned, and after five days of cruising about, 449 put into Guadalcanal on April 12. A few days later Kennedy, ready to disembark after more than a month at sea, was standing at the rail off Tulagi, reflecting on a large billboard that Admiral William F. Halsey had ordered to be erected on the commanding hillside. The message fairly screamed at Kennedy and other newcomers:

KILL JAPS. KILL JAPS.
KILL MORE JAPS.

You will help to kill the yellow
bastards if you do your job well.

TWO

AMONG THE SCORES of ships and small craft scattered about the palm-fringed harbor at Tulagi was PT 109, a grimy, battle-scarred, rat-ridden, cockroach-infested veteran of the Guadalcanal campaign.

Scarcely nine months before, in July 1942, PT 109, a trim new eighty-foot plywood speedboat with four torpedo tubes, machine guns and an anti-aircraft gun, had been plopped into the oily waters of Newark Bay. In the cluttered shipyard of the Elco Naval Division of the Electric Boat Company in Bayonne, New Jersey, the Navy unceremoniously took possession. Lt. (jg) Bryant L. Larson of Minneapolis turned up with a crew. The men looked the boat over with satisfaction and started her three twelve-cylinder Packard engines.

With Lt. Larson at the wheel the saga of PT 109 began with a winding run through the reeking, sooty, flat industrial waste-lands of New Jersey. She swept past smoking factories and the rusty hulls of freighters tied up at docks, under the blackened bridge of the Jersey Central, through a landscape littered with industry's contribution—pig iron, fuel oil, chemicals, rails and vehicles—to the might of a nation at war.

PT 109, carving a graceful bow wave and a gleaming white wake through the dirty water, recalled man's contribution. Her prow was high. Her radio antenna swayed in the wind. Her torpedo tubes pointed out to sea. Against the backdrop of factories and oil tanks she was a smoothly gliding symbol of the gallantry, dash, daring, even recklessness without which pig iron and kilowatts would have been useless.

From Newark Bay 109 ran through the Kill Van Kull into New York Bay. Passing the Statue of Liberty she picked up speed and headed for the Navy Yard in Brooklyn. A few days later she began her shakedown cruises back and forth through the East River, Long Island Sound and Narragansett Bay, plying between Brooklyn and the PT training center at Melville.

Riding the new boat at high speed was an exhilarating bout with wind and spray. In waves the bottom slapped the water so hard a sailor had to keep his balance with the spring in his knees, like a skier on a bumpy slope. For the crew of 109 it was fine sport dashing through the Sound at forty miles an hour or more, as if racing in to fire a "fish" at an enemy ship and then zigzagging away to escape retribution.

The boat performed well. It was powerful, seaworthy and maneuverable, though not quite so fast as some other PTs of the same class, or so Lt. Larson thought. By the end of summer 109 was ready. The crew drove her to Norfolk whence she was shipped to Balboa, Panama, for further training as part of Motor Torpedo Boat Squadron 5. Then in September she was transferred to Squadron 2 and loaded aboard a Liberty ship bound for Nouméa. From there she was towed by an old four-stack destroyer to Tulagi and was soon sent into action in the waters north of Guadalcanal.

One night 109 searched the Cape Esperance area and returned with three holes in her hull from shore batteries. Another night she patrolled off Lunga Point. Later she slipped into Savo Island with supplies for the Army. Sometimes she carried mail to the troops. These were typical of her missions in the winter of 1943. Once she refused to start at all, and thereby saved her own life. Unable to get the engines going on this particular night, Lt. Rollin E. Westholm, Squadron Commander, transferred the crew to PT 112, which had not been given a mission, and patrolled between Cape Esperance and Doma Cove. Early in the morning of January 11 he led a three-boat attack on four Japanese destroyers. The destroyer *Hatsukaze* was damaged by torpedoes, but PT 112 went to the bottom with shell holes in her hull and engine-room bulkhead. Lt. Westholm and his men, two of them wounded by shrapnel, took to a life raft and were rescued at dawn by another PT boat.

Lt. Westholm had 109 back in operation in time to get shot at again by the enemy forty-eight hours later. One night PT 109 went to the rescue of some Japanese sailors whose ship had been sunk under them. The crew managed to take all aboard but one. This one, an officer, swam furiously to evade capture. Finally, Lt. Westholm got the idea of cornering him with bullets. He drew his Colt .45 and fired just ahead of the swimmer. Gradually he was forcing the man in against the boat when a motor machinist's mate emerged from the engine-room hatch and saw the bullets striking the water near the Japanese. Evidently concluding that Westholm was an atrocious marksman, the "motor-mac" picked up a rifle and with a single shot put a bullet through the swimmer's head.

In February Lt. Westholm was promoted to chief staff officer to Commander Allen P. Calvert, commanding officer of the Motor Torpedo Boat Flotilla at Tulagi, and in April Lt. Larson came due for rotation home. On April 25, 1943, the log of PT 109 contained this entry:

0830   Underway for Sesapi[†]
1100   Lt. (jg) J. F. Kennedy assumed command of the boat
1145   Moored at usual berth in bushes

[†]Sesape, the PT base on Tulagi.

ONE DAY IN THE SUMMER of 1941 Jack Kennedy had sailed into Edgartown, on Martha's Vineyard, at the tiller of his centerboard sloop *Victura*. An ardent sailor since the time he was so small his parents on the shore could barely see his head above the gunwales of a sailboat in the water, Kennedy often sailed from Hyannis Port across Nantucket Sound to Martha's Vineyard.

On this trip, however, he saw a sight which particularly caught his fancy and the memory of which was to beckon him in the future. When he entered the harbor he beheld a new PT boat that the Navy had brought over from Newport and put on exhibition.

In World War I, Britain, Italy and Germany had employed motor torpedo boats, and since the beginning of World War II the British had been using them again with good results. However, "mosquito boats," as they were often called then, were a new wrinkle for Americans. High Navy brass in Washington was said to have opposed their development by the United States, but President Roosevelt and General Douglas MacArthur prevailed. General MacArthur thought motor torpedo boats would be effective in the waters around the Philippines, and events were soon to prove him right.

In any case the trim lines and scrappy look of the PT boat at Edgartown aroused young Kennedy's imagination. When he inspected her he had an urge to climb behind the wheel and open the throttles wide.

Actually, Kennedy had not had a great deal of experience with motorboats. Sailing was his joy. When he was a boy his father bought a sixteen-foot Wianno Jr. with a jib and mainsail. In those days Mr. and Mrs. Kennedy had eight children, so they named the boat *Tenovus*. After Edward was born in 1932 the elder Kennedy bought a second Wianno Jr. and named her *Onemore*. During those years he also bought the *Victura* and a Star boat, *Flash II*.

One year Jack Kennedy won the Nantucket Sound championship in the Star boat class. Also, he sailed on the Harvard

crew that won the McMillan Trophy for the Eastern inter-
collegiate championship. In summers he and his brother Joe
used to race every chance they got. Sometimes they alternated
as skipper. At other times they competed against each other.

Despite these salt-water adventures, however, Jack Kennedy
went to the Army to enlist when the crisis was approaching
before Pearl Harbor. He was rejected because of a sprain of the
lower back suffered while he was playing junior varsity football
at Harvard. Undaunted, he buckled down to remedial exercises
for five months, and then tried the Navy. In September 1941
he passed a fitness test and in October was appointed an ensign
in the United States Naval Reserve.

He was ordered to active duty at the Pentagon. He was
assigned to Navy intelligence and helped prepare a daily news
digest. In his spare time he took correspondence courses in
intelligence and in Navy regulations and customs. On Sunday,
December 7, he and his friend LeMoyne Billings went to Grif-
fith Stadium and watched Sammy Baugh pass the Washington
Redskins to a 20–14 victory over the Philadelphia Eagles. Riding home afterward they heard the news that the Japanese had
attacked Pearl Harbor. Kennedy immediately applied for sea
duty. Instead, to his disappointment, he was transferred, in January 1942, to the headquarters of the 6th Naval District in
Charleston, South Carolina. There he was put to work on a program for protecting war plants from enemy bombing, an assignment that bored him nearly to death.

In the summer of 1942 Ensign Kennedy was sent to the
Naval Reserve Officers' Training School at Northwestern University, and there his career at last took a more exciting turn.

One of the early American heroes of World War II was Lt.
John D. Bulkeley, who won the Medal of Honor for his role as
commander of Motor Torpedo Boat Squadron 3. This famed
squadron had evacuated General MacArthur from the Philippines, sunk an auxiliary Japanese cruiser in Subic Bay and per-

formed such other daredevil feats as to make PT boats just about the most glamorous weapon in the American arsenal as far as the public was concerned. *They Were Expendable*, the book about the exploits of Bulkeley and Lt. Robert B. Kelly, another Squadron 3 hero, was a best-seller and had everyone talking about the marvels of PT boats and their brave crews. After the Subic Bay affair the Tokyo radio reported that the Americans had a secret weapon, a monster that roared, flapped its wings and fired torpedoes in all directions.

These epics were reviving Ensign Kennedy's memory of the boat he saw at Edgartown. He decided that he wanted to be a PT-boat skipper, and unexpectedly circumstances conspired to help him. After he got to Northwestern an announcement was made that Lt. Bulkeley and Lt. John Harllee,[†] senior instructor at Melville, would visit the campus and interview candidates for the PT service. Ensign Kennedy sprang at the opportunity.

As it turned out, the qualifications Bulkeley and Harllee were looking for he had in ample measure. Among other things they wanted young men who had done well in their studies, who were athletic and who had had extensive experience in handling small craft. This last requirement was one of the reasons why so many young PT officers were Ivy Leaguers who had enjoyed the luxury of owning their own boats or of growing up around yacht clubs and racing in someone else's. Ensign Kennedy had done well at Harvard. He had been a member of the Harvard swimming team, which impressed Bulkeley and Harllee. And, of course, his long experience with sailboats was a capital asset.

Bulkeley and Harllee recommended Ensign Kennedy as a PT officer, and on October 1, 1942, he began the eight-week training course at Melville.

The Motor Torpedo Boat Squadron Training Center was on

[†]In 1961 President Kennedy nominated Rear Admiral John Harllee as a member of the Maritime Commission.

Narragansett Bay. Officers and men lived in Quonset huts and
took courses in gunnery, navigation, seamanship, engineering
and the handling of torpedoes. A good deal of the training was
done on PT boats. It was a robust life with early reveille, followed
by calisthenics and running. Athletics were obligatory. It was fall,
and Ensign Kennedy turned out for touch football at the first
opportunity. Seeing him approach in a black sweater with a red
"H," Ensign George Ross, of Highland Park, Illinois, whose
fate was one day to be closely intertwined with his, thought
Kennedy was a youth from the Hun School. He did not look
old enough to Ross to have been admitted to Melville. On
weekends Kennedy would invite fellow officers from his hut to
join him for touch football and walks on the shore in Hyannis
Port, which was not far away.

In October Kennedy was promoted to lieutenant, junior
grade, and at the end of November he finished his course. He
hoped to be assigned at once to a squadron that was in action
somewhere. Lt. Harllee, however, wanted him as an instructor
because of his record. He had been graded as superior in ship-
handling, good in engineering and other technical subjects and
"very willing and conscientious." Accordingly, he was assigned
to MTB Squadron 4, the base squadron at Melville, and was
made skipper of PT 101, a boat then being used for training.

Kennedy was disappointed at remaining in Melville, but he
took his new responsibilities seriously. One day he was going
out on a training cruise for a group of officer-students. His crew
was to have included Ensign Paul B. Fay, Jr., of San Francisco.
PT 101 was an older seventy-seven-foot boat and Ensign Fay had
some friends going out on the same cruise in one of the new
Elco eighty-footers. He thought he would enjoy that more. So
he sent word to 101 by semaphore that he would be traveling
in the other boat. Somehow the message was not understood,
and 101 left with the redheaded Fay listed as absent. Back on
shore a few hours later, Kennedy chewed him out with an

intensity that left Fay limp. Fay knew damn good and well what his assignment was. Why wasn't he there? What if everybody in the Navy bounced into any boat that caught his fancy? Multiply this boner several million times. Where would the country stand in the war if all men behaved this way?

Kennedy crowned Ensign Fay's ordeal by telling him that he thought he would have to recommend his dismissal from the PT service. Ensign Fay pleaded with Kennedy, he acknowledged that he had done a foolish thing, and assured Kennedy that he had learned his lesson. Lt. Kennedy did not withdraw his threat, and Fay had to leave with it hanging over him. Still he had a feeling that Kennedy would not recommend his dismissal, and his hunch proved right.[†]

Kennedy was living in a Quonset hut, bunked between Ensign John L. Iles of Baton Rouge and Lt. (jg) Torbert H. Macdonald,[††] the former Harvard football star, who had been Kennedy's college roommate and whom Kennedy had lured to Melville. With the coming of winter, Ensign Iles shivered in bed at night and wished he was back in Louisiana. Kennedy showed him how to keep a little warmer by putting newspapers under his mattress.

With winter also came the news that some of the boats, including Kennedy's, were moving out. They would be driven to Jacksonville and then shipped to Panama. Passing North Carolina, one of the boats ran aground. Kennedy went to her assistance in PT 101. He threw over a line, but as he started to tow the other boat, the rope got caught in one of his own propellers, and he dived overboard to clear it. The water almost froze him. By the time the squadron reached Jacksonville he had a high

---

[†]Not only did Lt. Kennedy refrain from recommending Fay's dismissal from PT service but in 1961 President Kennedy nominated Fay as Under Secretary of the Navy.

[††]Now Representative Macdonald, Democrat, of Massachusetts.

fever and had to go to a hospital for several days. He put in a
long-distance call to Lt. Macdonald, who was always telling him
how cold the water is in Maine.

"It's colder in North Carolina," Kennedy said.

Meanwhile he had been told that the boats he was with were
going to stay in Panama for a long time. In desperation he and
his father went to work on some high Navy officers the
Kennedys had known while at the embassy in London. Their
intercession did the trick. Instead of going to Panama, Kennedy
was pulled out and ordered to the Solomon Islands as an officer replacement.

THREE

TULAGI, THE PREWAR CAPITAL of the British Solomon Islands Protectorate, was seized by the Japanese five months after Pearl Harbor and recaptured by Americans as part of the operation of the invasion of Guadalcanal in August 1942. It is a narrow, hilly island that lies aslant off the southwest coast of Florida Island, which is many times larger. Among the repair shops, Quonset huts and the thatched-roofed officers' club called the Royal Palm were colonial landmarks like the rugby field and Government House.

The PT boss in the South Pacific, Commander Calvert, had his headquarters in "Calvertville" on Florida Island opposite the west bank of Tulagi. Calvertville contained a miscellany of native thatched huts, an old marine railway built by Chinese, a torpedo overhaul shop and a gateway with a sign, THRU THESE PORTALS PASS THE BEST M.T.B. FLOTILLA IN THE WORLD.

Most of the PT base operations, however, were centered across the channel from Calvertville in the old Chinese trading village of Sesape on Tulagi. Destroyers, Liberty ships, New Zealand corvettes steamed endlessly up and down the channel. PT boats rumbled about awaiting their turn in the floating drydock or nestled up to the PT tender *Jamestown* for minor repairs. When the PTs were not on the move they were moored under the bushes along the Tulagi or Florida shore to hide them from Japanese planes.

Kennedy had to wait only a short time for his assignment. When he was informed that he was to become the captain of PT 109, he promptly looked up her skipper, Lt. Larson, to whom he was the most welcome sight on earth. Larson had never laid eyes on him before, but he had a very warm spot in his heart for him because Kennedy's arrival meant that he could go home. The retiring skipper took his replacement down to the boat, and Kennedy rode with Larson a few times to familiarize himself with 109. Then Larson said good-by, and the new skipper was on his own.

Along with Larson went the old crew, with the exception of one officer who had only recently come aboard. Kennedy thus had the task not only of rehabilitating 109 but of selecting a new crew and welding boat and men into a tolerably efficient fighting unit in time for the offensive that was coming in the summer.

The hold-over from the old crew was Ensign Leonard J. Thom of Sandusky, Ohio, a capable and warmhearted giant, who looked like a Viking who had lost his way and sailed into the South Pacific by mistake. Ensign Thom had played left tackle on Francis Schmidt's team at Ohio State in 1939 and 1940. He was blond and grew a blond beard in the Navy. He was tall and broad-chested and had massive arms and shoulders. A number of athletes had gravitated to the PT service and whenever any of them became too obstreperous from grapefruit juice and 190-proof torpedo fluid the call went out for Thom, who could handle them without much difficulty. Kennedy made him executive officer of the boat. In time he was to become a close friend in whom the skipper would place great trust.

Kennedy picked his crew from among replacements who had recently arrived from Melville. Three of his men reported the same day he took command.

One was Gunner's Mate 2/c Charles A. Harris, a slight, dark-complexioned, wiry man of twenty, who was born in Watertown, outside Boston. Naturally, everyone called him "Bucky" Harris after the former manager of the Red Sox. As a boy he had spent a lot of time around the water. After graduating from Watertown High School he got a job with Hood Rubber and when the war began he enlisted in the Navy.

Motor Machinist's Mate 2/c Leon E. Drawdy was ten years older than Harris. A tall, lanky man with a long, narrow face and a kindly manner, he spoke with a deep, drawling voice and had the rare habit of thinking out what he was going to say before he said it. Before World War I his family had owned a considerable amount of land in his native Florida, but had lost it through tax liens after his father died in 1918. At the time of Pearl Harbor Drawdy was working as a machinist in Chicago.

The third man who came aboard that day was Motor Machinist's Mate 2/c Edmund T. Drewitch. He was thirty, the same age as Drawdy, and his home was Pittsburgh. His father had made him learn to play the piano almost as soon as he could walk, and when he was ten he accompanied his brother, Chester, a violinist, at a church recital. By the time he was in high school he had his own nine-piece jazz band called the Campus Clowns. Later he tried studying law at night, but was working as a steel inspector for Jones & Laughlin when the war began. Ed Drewitch was the crew's politician. He was quick and resourceful and seemed to know his way about.

Gunner's Mate 3/c Maurice L. Kowal and Torpedoman 2/c Andrew Jackson Kirksey reported for duty on May 1.

Kowal was a whimsical, companionable man of twenty-one, who was regarded by some of his mates as their leading wit. He was born of Polish immigrant parents in Ware, Massachusetts, but grew up in Uxbridge, not far from Boston. When the war began he was working in a factory that built engines for Victory ships.

Kirksey had a quiet manner and pleasant disposition. He was a native of Reynolds, Georgia, and had gone to school in Columbus, Georgia, through the tenth grade. He was working as a refrigeration engineer at the time he enlisted in Macon on July 1, 1942. Now at the age of twenty-five he had one son, Jack, born to his wife, Cloye Ann, three months after he had enlisted.

Radioman 2/c John E. Maguire, twenty-six, joined the crew on May 5. He was a native of Dobbs Ferry, New York, and grew up on the banks of the Hudson. In the springtime he and other boys used to go swimming in the nude along the New York Central tracks, where they had to dive into the river every time a train appeared. After Pearl Harbor his brother, William, joined the Navy and volunteered for the PT service. He liked it so well that he persuaded John to give up his job with Anaconda Wire & Cable and follow him. William as well as John wound up on PTs in the South Pacific.

The next recruit was Seaman 1/c Edgar E. Mauer, twenty-eight, who reported only a few days after his first ship, the PT tender *Niagara*, formerly Tommy Manville's yacht, had been sunk under him by Japanese bombers near San Cristobal. When Mauer first saw his new skipper with the thin, handsome young face, high cheekbones and unruly shock of hair, he was dismayed.

"Another ninety-day wonder, eh?" he asked one of the sailors whose name he did not yet know.

"Oh, yeah?" the man replied sarcastically. "Well, you'll find out."

When the *Niagara* was sunk Mauer was rescued without any possessions but the clothes he was wearing. Supplies were so short then that when he reported to 109 he did not even have a seabag. "We'll have to do something about this," Kennedy told him. The skipper left the ship and went to the Navy stores where he was able to get Mauer a shirt and a change of underwear. There were no shoes Mauer's size, so Kennedy went around to the Marines and talked them out of not only a pair of shoes, some dungarees, shirts, socks and underwear for Mauer but a couple of pairs of shoes for some of the other men.

"Say, we don't have a cook aboard," he told Mauer. "Can you cook?"

Mauer replied that when he was a boy in St. Louis he and his brothers had had to take turns cooking at home. "I can do short-order cooking," he said.

"Well, that's good enough for me," Kennedy said. And Mauer became PT 109's jack-of-all-trades—quartermaster, signalman, cook, among them. There were to be mealtimes when Kennedy would wonder whether quartermaster and signalman wouldn't have been enough.

The new skipper of PT 109 made his first log entry on April 26. It was modest enough, reading in its entirety:

0800   moored in usual berth
John F. Kennedy
Lt. (jg) USNR

Without waiting for all of his crew to report, Kennedy set to work on repairs and training. At this point the new skipper was less than an old salt himself, and the men were atrociously green. On one of the first days he came jauntily down to the boat twirling his index finger over his head in a wind-her-up signal. After a struggle the best the men could do was to get one of the three engines going. Indeed the condition of the engines might have defied more seasoned hands. Kennedy's command was only a few days old when he began to feel like the PT men in New Guinea who sang,

> Oh, some PTs do seventy-five
> And some do sixty-nine.
> When we get ours to run at all
> We think we're doing fine.

Accustomed to the clean new boats at Melville, the men were taken aback by the dirt and grime of a boat that had been in combat in the tropics for months. When 109 was moored at the shore, the heavy jungle bushes concealed her from enemy planes, as was intended, but also bridged the way for formidable boarding parties of rats and cockroaches. Once there was a dreadful stench aboard, which nobody could account for until someone found part of a dead fish that a rat had left under a step.

The new men were so unsure of themselves even at the jobs for which they had been trained that when Lt. Kennedy ordered the boat to sea for some test-firing, Gunner's Mate Harris was frightened. Although he knew enough about the guns, he had never fired one without an instructor at his side.

One day when 109 had returned to Tulagi from a practice run, the crew was terrified by the sudden roar of the twin .50-caliber machine guns in the forward turret. Some of the men thought Japanese planes had slipped through. Jerking around, they saw Gunner's Mate Kowal desperately clutching the guns and looking more scared than if the sky were dark with Nips. While cleaning the weapons Kowal had accidentally set them off, and tracers streaking across the harbor sent sailors diving to the decks.

When the noise of the guns finally stopped, the noise of Kennedy's enraged voice in the cockpit just below shattered the air all over again. Fortunately, a safety bar had prevented Kowal from cleaning the guns with the barrels pointing into the cockpit.

When her turn came PT 109 went into drydock, and Kennedy donned shorts and worked with the men in scraping the bottom, cleaning the bilge, sandpapering and putting on a fresh coat of paint. For camouflage in the waterways among the islands the boat was painted forest green. One morning while a carpenter was doing some work on the exterior of the hull below the gunwale, out of sight from the deck, Lt. Kennedy emerged from below with a pail of dirty water and tossed the water over the side. No sooner had it disappeared than the dripping face of an enraged man glared over the gunwale.

"Why don't you watch what the hell you're doing?" the man bawled.

"Oh, I *am* sorry," Lt. Kennedy apologized. After trying his best to pacify the man he went below again.

"Do you know who that was you were talking to?" Radioman Maguire asked the carpenter.

"No," he snapped. "Who?"

"That was the skipper of this boat," Maguire informed him.

"Oh, Lord!" the man said.

After several days PT 109 was back in good enough shape again to begin taking her turn on night patrols. Although to the new crew everything that stirred was a Japanese ship or plane, there was no action of any consequence out of Tulagi at that time. The patrols were largely precautionary, intended to make sure that no Japanese ships would attempt hit-and-run attacks on Guadalcanal.

Lt. Kennedy's log sketched a laconic picture of 109's activities at sea in May. Thus:

MAY 8

1820   Left Sesapi [*sic*] in company of PT 59 for patrol Savo Island to Cape Esperance—visibility nearly zero.

MAY 13

0045   0145—Repeated flashes thought to be gun-fire seen in Russel [*sic*] Islands area.

MAY 17

0040   White light seen from center of Savo Island.

MAY 21

2030 Fired 10 rounds 30 calibre at floating oil drums.

MAY 23

0530 Left patrol area for base—Sesapi—
0540 Flares from anti-aircraft seen—apparently friendly.
2130 Red light seen on surface of water—bearing 30°—
      distance 4 miles PT 109 investigated. Results negative.

Life at Tulagi wasn't ideal, but it was far from intolerable as war went. Japanese attacks were limited to periodic sorties by "Washing-machine Charlies," the planes whose unsynchronized engines sounded like something down in the laundry. Charlie's raids often forced the exasperated crew of 109 to dump oil drums overboard while refueling in order to scamper to open water as regulations required. This was a sweaty nuisance, but the plane was less feared by the men than the falling shrapnel from American guns that hammered away at Charlie.

The comparative freedom from danger was only part of the picture. The food was monotonous. The weather was miserably hot and uncomfortable. Recreation was almost nonexistent for the men, at least in the beginning.

Kennedy lived ashore in Sesape. When he had first arrived he ran into his old Melville Quonset-hut mate, Ensign Iles, who had got to Tulagi ahead of him and found an empty native thatched hut behind the Navy reefer boxes (large refrigerators). Ensign Iles suggested that they fix the place up and live in it when they were not needed on their boats. Together they scrounged some planks for flooring, cleaned the hut out, and brought in a few orange crates to put their clothes in. For an air-raid shelter whenever Condition Red was ordered they used the space between two of the reefer boxes.

Best of all, or so they thought, they somehow acquired a young Melanesian houseboy named Lami. The Melanesians in the Solomon Islands had long been accustomed to British rule, and when war descended on them, they became friendly and helpful to the Americans as allies of the British. Melanesians tend to be short of stature. They have dark kinky hair, and their skin is very black. Even their lips and eyes are black. Against such a background, their teeth seem blindingly white.

Lami proved a handy fellow, and at night he used to sleep on the floor between Kennedy and Iles. One day he confided to them that he had once been a cannibal. The two surprised officers were well aware that the Solomons had a long history of cannibalism and head-hunting. However, they were not sure whether to take Lami's claim seriously. They taught him to play catch and made a fairly good volley-ball player of him. Still his past raised some disturbing questions. Iles prodded him about it.

"Me ate the padre," he said mysteriously.

When Ensign Thom moved into the hut, Lami seemed to look very peculiarly—perhaps hungrily—at his massive blond frame. Then one day Lami simply vanished. Kennedy, Thom and Iles could only learn that some New Zealand authorities had come and taken Lami away.

Kennedy passed his free time at Sesape reading—he had a copy of Tolstoy's *War and Peace* with him—playing an occasional game of poker or cribbage and participating in the debates that went on endlessly on every conceivable subject.

A rumor had cropped up, for example, that the United States was going to pay Australian plantation owners for coconut palms that had been destroyed on Tulagi and other islands by American shells. Lt. (jg) Sidney Rabekoff, of New York, declared that any such payment would be outrageous. The United States, he argued, was pouring dollars and lives into the recapture of the islands. This was payment enough, he said. Kennedy disagreed, arguing that the plantations were private property and that the owners were justified in seeking compensation for their destruction.

On April 18 Kennedy had taken his boat on a mission to Guadalcanal and was standing on Henderson Field when the Lightnings that had just shot down Fleet Admiral Isoroku Yamamoto, Commander-in-Chief of the Combined Japanese Fleet, returned from Bougainville. Kennedy watched as Captain Thomas G. Lanphier, the pilot who bagged Yamamoto's plane, did a roll over the field in exultation.

On the night of May 21 a political debate got raging in a tent. Lt. Alvin P. Cluster, a Missouri Republican, filled the air with denunciations of Roosevelt and the New Deal. Kennedy, whom Lt. Cluster had not yet met, argued with him persistently, defending the Administration point by point. In the usual course someone got off a potshot at Mrs. Roosevelt for good measure. Kennedy retorted that he had been to Washington and had met Mrs. Roosevelt. She was, he said, very different in person from her portrayal in newspapers and was very charming.

To cap it all Lt. Cluster jumped on Franklin Roosevelt for giving rich men the prize ambassadorships, a point that Kennedy let pass. Presently, Cluster felt one of the other officers tugging at his sleeve. Managing to get him aside, his friend asked, "Don't you think you are being a little rough on Kennedy?"

"Why Kennedy?" Lt. Cluster inquired.

His friend explained why, and Lt. Cluster promptly abandoned this line of argument.

Through incidents like this, Kennedy's identity sooner or later became known practically wherever he went. One evening when he was walking alone through a grove in Sesape, he was stopped by a tall, red-haired lieutenant, junior grade, who introduced himself as Edward F. McLaughlin, Jr.[†]

Lt. McLaughlin said that his father, the fire commissioner of Boston, was an old friend of Joseph P. Kennedy and of Kennedy's celebrated grandfather, former Mayor John F. (Honey

---

[†]Presently Lieutenant Governor of Massachusetts.

Fitz) Fitzgerald, of Boston, who had often visited the McLaughlin home.

Honey Fitz, still flourishing at the age of eighty, had been one of the robust and picturesque figures in Boston in the last years of the old century and the early years of the new. He was sometimes the rival and sometimes the ally of Kennedy's paternal grandfather, Patrick J. Kennedy, who was variously fire commissioner, street commissioner, election commissioner, state representative, state senator and, above all, one of the coalition of Democratic bosses who picked candidates and generally ran Boston. Honey Fitz was famous for his rendition of "Sweet Adeline" and for turning up at weddings, even when uninvited, in a top hat and morning coat. His love of life and politics had exerted an influence on young Jack Kennedy, whom he used to take to Red Sox games and to the swan boats in the Public Garden. The two young lieutenants chatted about Boston and their families, and they became good friends.

In the Navy, or at least in that part of it in which he served, a much-used word in those historic times was "shafted." The word had several meanings. One of them had roughly the same connotation as "We wuz robbed." "Shafted" in this sense became a word greatly favored by Kennedy. Instead of saying that he had had dismal luck or had got a raw deal, he would mutter, "I was shafted."

Now there were many strange sounds that fell upon American ears in the South Pacific. There were parrots and parakeets and myna birds and screaming cockatoos, to mention only a few. But no sound was more memorable than "shafted," as uttered in Kennedy's Boston-Harvard accent. It lingered in the ear long after the broad *a* had died away in the breeze, and it imbedded itself so deeply in the consciousness of those who heard it that inevitably, as such things go, Kennedy became known as "Shafty."

The nickname had originated at Melville with Ensign Joe G. Atkinson, of Lebanon, Tennessee, who was a class behind

Kennedy. Atkinson, left guard and captain of the Vanderbilt football team of 1941, hit upon it when Kennedy, within his hearing, strode into a Quonset hut and told Lt. Macdonald, "I've
been shafted!" This was his complaint about being assigned as an
instructor instead of being shipped overseas. The nickname first
appeared in print in the South Pacific daubed on the warhead of
one of PT 109's torpedoes.

Toward the end of May PT 109 was shipshape, and skipper
and crew alike were becoming seasoned in their jobs. The boat
went out for drills and maneuvers of various sorts and practiced
riding in formation with other PTs. Test-firing by day and patrols
by night noticeably increased the efficiency of the men. As indi-
viduals they grew more confident, as a crew they became more
cohesive. They got to know one another and learned how to
live together in the tightly cramped quarters of a PT boat.

Kennedy spent a good deal of time aboard the boat, and his
men liked him. They thought he did a fair share of the work.
They found that he treated them much more like equals than
some other officers treated their crews. He was never dictatorial.
In particular the crew was grateful for his nonchalance toward
Navy regulations and Annapolis men.

Now deeply tanned, he usually went about stripped to the
waist, wearing a sheath knife in his belt, sun glasses and any one
of a variety of headgear. Although he was one day to become
known as a man who shunned hats, in the South Pacific they
were an obsession with him. He jealously hoarded a collection
of sun helmets, Navy hats, Army and Marine fatigue hats, baseball caps and yachting caps of all kinds, some with visors a foot
long. Drawdy once got an Army cap and offered to trade it for
one of Kennedy's baseball caps, but Kennedy would not swap.
Once a hat went into his collection no bargain or trade could
dislodge it.

As was often the case on small craft, skipper and crew were
companionable. Together they used to speculate on the hazards

that lay ahead of them and talk about what they would do under various circumstances. One problem they discussed, as some of them would particularly remember later on, was how they would react to the danger of capture by the enemy, if it should ever come. The stories of Japanese atrocities at this stage of the war were horrible, and from the beginning, it seems, the sentiment on 109 was against ever submitting to capture.

The crew found the skipper responsive to their feelings. During the early days at Tulagi, for example, they had taken a hearty dislike to a certain motormac who had been assigned a berth on the boat. At sea one night Kennedy gave some signal to the engine room to which there was no response. He slipped down to see what was the matter and to his astonishment found no one on duty. He had three motormacs aboard, and all of them were asleep. Bursting in on Drewitch's dreams, he demanded to know what kind of Navy this was supposed to be. Drewitch spluttered that he and Drawdy and the third motormac had divided the watch and that it was the third man's time to be on. Kennedy then woke the fellow, who disputed Drewitch. Drewitch flew into a rage and tried to punch him, but Kennedy separated them. Drawdy awoke, very much upset over the affair, and corroborated Drewitch's explanation. That was the end of 109 for the third motormac.

One thing that life at Tulagi was beginning to teach the crew was that all the glamorous literature back home about PT boats dashing out and torpedoing cruisers neglected to mention that a PT sailor in a place like the Solomons had a varied diet—varied, that is, to the extent of the cook's genius with Spam. To those who may have joined the Navy in preference to the Army because the Navy was reputed to serve better food it was becoming quite clear that a PT boat was not a battleship or an aircraft carrier. There were no spacious refrigerators full of meat, milk, butter, eggs and vegetables. More than one of the crew of 109 was to live to read and approve James A. Michener's observation in *Tales of the South Pacific*: "I have become damned sick and tired of the eyewash written about PT boats. . . . It was just dirty work, thumping, hammering, kidney-wrecking work. Even for strong guys from Montana it was rugged living." No bakery was aboard. In fact bread was often as scarce as beefsteak.

Seaman Mauer did his best. He served Spam as Spam, as Spamburgers, as hash with slices of pickle. It took the most diligent scrounging by sturdy talents such as Kennedy and his men soon manifested to find anything better than a fare of Spam à la Mauer, canned Vienna sausage and baked beans.

Occasionally they caught a grouper for a change of diet. They discovered that by firing a rifle or dropping a hand grenade into a school of fish they could stun enough of them to make a sizable catch. Often, however, they did not know what kind of fish they were getting, and tales told about poisonous fish frequently caused them to throw their catch back into the water untasted.

Other forms of ingenuity were displayed, not always with satisfactory results. One night Drawdy contrived to slip into a mess tent at Sesape and make off with what he believed to be a gallon of peaches. When he opened the can in the presence of a hungry crew, the loot turned out to be spinach, and it was promptly heaved overboard.

Kennedy's craving for sweets kept him on the prowl a good deal of the time. Whenever he thought it would do any good he made the rounds of Army PXs in the region or a sortie into a Seabee camp. If he didn't have any money, which was frequently the case, he would borrow some from his men until the next payday. Occasionally their loans would bring a magnificent harvest, as the skipper would show up with a box of twenty-four O. Henrys. When a cargo ship appeared on the horizon Kennedy would sometimes rev up 109 and race out to meet her to beg, borrow or buy fresh food. Now and then he would return triumphantly with a dozen eggs or a loaf of bread or a couple of bars of soap.

In particular Kennedy was a fiend for hotcakes. An angry cook once ran him out of a chow line in Sesape for coming back for seconds, and the crew teased him about his sweet tooth.

"When we get back to the States," Drawdy promised him one day, "we'll have Mauer cook hotcakes for you every day."

He cooked them every day that flour was available. Sticking to the recipe his mother had taught him years ago, Mauer would throw together dried eggs, powdered milk, flour and canned shortening or "nonperishable butter," as it was called. Once Kennedy had doughnuts on board another PT but when he asked his cook to try them, Mauer shook his head morosely. This was something his mother had not got around to.

The crew especially admired Kennedy's genius for "promoting" powdered ice cream. How he managed to keep the supply flowing was a marvel to them. The powder was mixed with water and placed in ice-cube trays in the boat's small refrigerator. When it froze it made tolerably good ice cream, and the skipper used to eat dishes of it at night as he piloted 109 here and there through the South Seas.

The enlisted men had resources of their own in the great South Pacific art of scrounging. For a PT man to get on a work crew unloading a cargo ship was meat on the table, a dream come true, the camel's nose under the tent. One afternoon Maguire managed to make himself available to help unload a hundred cases of beer onto a ramp lighter. From long experience the Navy was well aware of the hazards surrounding a cargo of this splendor. Accordingly, a check system was instituted whereby one case of beer shuttled from the ship to the lighter to the beach became one case of beer checked off on the beach, two cases of beer handed from the ship to the lighter to the beach were two cases of beer checked off on the beach. Maguire, however, was on board the lighter and he worked with

the devotion of a man who knew what was expected of him in
the war effort. He noticed as he passed the cases along that the
engine was housed in a boxlike structure with a lid. With his
foot he raised the lid, placed a case of beer inside, lowered the
lid, and passed along the next case to the "bucket brigade."

When the last case was on the beach, the supply officer called
out in anguish, "We've only got ninety-nine cases. We're missing
one!"

"Not one of you is coming ashore until we have a hundred
cases here!"

This put in motion a great snooping all over the place. Every
time someone neared the engine housing, a butterfly fluttered in
Maguire's stomach, but somehow no one ever thought to lift the
lid. It was late and the supply officer knew the men had to be
getting back to the boats. In frustration he conceded against his
better judgment that there may have been only ninety-nine
cases after all.

Maguire hung around for a long time waiting for the coxswain to leave the lighter. When he showed no sign of leaving,
Maguire went aboard, gave him six cans of beer in return for a
promise of silence, and case No. 100, minus six cans, was finally
unloaded. Even today, this remains one of Maguire's fondest
war memories.

A new squadron arrived at Tulagi and innocently stacked its
supplies in neat piles on a dock. These supplies included fifteen
five-gallon cans of 190-proof torpedo fluid, much coveted in the
South Pacific for purposes other than firing torpedoes. PT 109
had come over to the dock to pick up some .50-caliber
machine-gun ammunition, and along with the bullets the men
picked up a can of alcohol. Other crews got word of the wind-
fall, and from all over the harbor, PT boats suddenly found it necessary to go to the dock on some mission or other. Before long
only five cans remained. When the officers of the new squadron
discovered what was happening, the greatest crisis since the

April 7 air raid descended on Tulagi. Frantic representations were made to Commander Calvert, and the base sent out official search parties to all the boats.

When the investigators boarded 109 they searched her from stem to stern, even the bilges, but they could not find a single can of alcohol. After the sleuths had gone the men climbed into a skiff and rowed up the line of bushes a short distance until they came to a cork floating on the surface. They lifted the cork, and a line came up with it. They pulled up the line, and a five-gallon can of alcohol emerged from the water.

Back on 109 again they opened the can and found that it contained "pink lady." The color was caused by a chemical introduced to make the fluid nonpotable. The men took the can down to the galley of the boat and poured the pink lady into a canteen. They fitted some copper tubing and coils into the canteen, placed the canteen on the hotplate, and ran the coils through cold water. At the end of the tubing they placed a tin cup to catch the drops of pure alcohol that would be redistilled from the pink lady. Mauer had some pineapple juice ready for the occasion.

The men supposed that their skipper was not altogether unaware of the cause of their pleasure, but he remained preoccupied with the higher purposes of the war.

When there were religious services in Sesape on Sundays, Kennedy, if he happened to be aboard 109, would ride over with Maguire. A whaleboat used to make the rounds of the PTs picking up men for church.

"The boat's here, Mr. Kennedy," Maguire would call. "Are you going to mass?"

Kennedy and Maguire would scramble aboard for the ride over to the chapel, which was made of straw.

Before leaving Tulagi Kennedy had occasion to take 109 to a machine shop at Calvertville, and as he was pulling away, he heard a shout of "Hey, Jack," from a passing whaleboat. Looking across the water he saw his friend from the *Rochambeau*, Ensign Reed, who had kept his word and volunteered for PTs in Nouméa. He had just arrived. The two would be together a good deal in the next few months.

The crew of PT 109 grew restless to move on. They were, in the vernacular of the day, "Tulagi-groggy." Had they known what awaited them to the west, perhaps they would have been satisfied with the uneventful patrol duty at Tulagi.

FOUR

AS A STEP on the long road to Tokyo the Joint Chiefs of Staff had ordered an invasion of the island of New Georgia in the Western Solomons. The New Georgia group consists of hundreds of small islands and several larger ones, including Rendova, Gizo, Kolombangara, Vella Lavella, Wana Wana, Arundel, Ganongga, Vangunu, Tetipari, Gatukai and, of course, New Georgia itself, which is much the largest. On its western tip, opposite Rendova, the Japanese had an important airstrip. D-Day was June 30, 1943.

By the end of May, Tulagi was astir with preparations for the offensive. Destroyers, cargo ships and landing craft of all sizes were moving up from Guadalcanal and the New Hebrides. At the same time many vessels that had been staging at Tulagi were being ordered on to the Russell Islands, which lay eighty miles to the west and about a third of the way to New Georgia.

The PT boats were among the first to leave. Most of them were bound for the Russells, but Commander Calvert received an order to send six to New Guinea. After five had been assigned, there was a question whether the sixth would be Kennedy's PT 109 or Lt. (jg) Pat Munroe's PT 110. Both skippers wanted the New Guinea assignment because the scuttlebutt was that there would be more action there. Lt. Munroe took out a coin and flipped it.

"Call it," he said.

"Tails," Kennedy called.

"Heads it is," Munroe said triumphantly.

That fifty-cent piece sent Munroe to New Guinea and Kennedy into the New Georgia campaign.

Kennedy was ordered to depart for the Russells at dawn on May 30. The trip was made with a bit more equipment than regulations called for. The night before, Maguire, Mauer, Kowal and Harris had gone ashore to an outdoor movie, returning in a dinghy with an outboard motor which they had scrounged. They hauled the dinghy up on the stern and hid it underneath a tarpaulin. Once they reached the Russell Islands, the crew of 109 sported a pleasure craft of its own and was the envy of all the other boats.

In the Russells muddy streams wind from the irregular shore line back into the emerald jungles. Exploring one of these streams in the dinghy, Harris and Kowal came upon crocodiles lurking along the banks or drifting menacingly in midstream. When the dinghy got close, they thrashed about viciously. After that the sailors organized crocodile hunts, heading straight for the crocodiles in the dinghy and either shooting them with rifles or blowing them up with hand grenades.

When there were no crocodiles around the sailors hunted parrots or fished. Once they caught an eel three feet long that put up such a wicked fight they were afraid to remove the hook from its mouth. Instead they tied the line to the boat with half the eel in the water and half out. When they went to have a second try at the hook the half of the eel that was in the water was gone.

Native villages were off limits to Americans. However, the explorations in the dinghy made the temptation to have a look at some of these strange places with thatched huts on stilts almost overpowering. One afternoon Kirksey, Kowal and Harris, seeing some grass shacks back in the jungle as they were cruising along, anchored close to the shore and climbed barefoot into about eight inches of water. They had taken only a couple of steps when they were aghast to discover that they were in a writhing tangle of ringed water snakes. Like three terrified kangaroos the men bounded ashore breathless with fright. Not a man among them could even imagine how he was going to get up the nerve to return to the dinghy.

When the three sailors entered the village the women disappeared, and silent, frowning, half-naked black men converged on the visitors, carrying spears. The Americans grinned and said hello, to which pleasantries the natives responded by thumping the handles of their spears on the ground and glaring. They did not attack the Americans, but they shoved aggressively forward, crowding them out of the village. The men were quite ready to leave and were dismayed when the hostile natives kept following them, thumping their spears.

This harassment continued all the way to the beach. When at last the unhappy sailors came to where their dinghy was anchored they were so eager to get aboard and shove off that they splashed through the water scarcely thinking about the snakes. It was not until they were safely back on board 109 that it occurred to them that in wading out they had noticed no snakes at all.

KENNEDY AND OTHER OFFICERS were living in a pleasant, weather-beaten old plantation house, which had broad front steps and a tin roof. It stood on stilts and looked out over Sunlight Channel, running north and south between the two islands that in the main make up the Russells—Pavuvu and Banika.

Behind the house grew a large lime tree, which the officers appreciated most whenever they could relax in the afternoon with a glass of lime juice and alcohol. Beyond the lime tree was a urinal in the form of Tojo's grave, complete with headstone.

Kennedy spent some of his spare hours playing cribbage. Moreover he had brought a record-player ashore, and he had one favorite record that he played so often that his roommates in their sleep could hear the words

> Blue skies
> Smiling at me,
> Nothing but blue skies
> Do I see . . .

The Russell Islands are shimmeringly beautiful, with lush jungles surrounding large coconut plantations cultivated before the war by Lever Brothers. The waters are a lovely blend of azure blue and emerald green. Below the surface the brilliant reds and blues and yellows of tropical fish blink against the multi-colored coral bottom. The Americans were fascinated by the rich fish life.

One day as 109 was pulling away from the base in a cove at the southern end of Sunlight Channel Kennedy was lying face downward on the bow peering into the water. All of a sudden he gave a shout for the crew, and looking over his shoulder the men saw a sight that was to haunt some of them in the near future. Swimming just off the prow on the port side was a large shark. Kennedy called to Maguire to speed the boat up. As she spurted forward, the shark shot ahead at the same speed, as if in tandem.

"Slow down," Kennedy called.

When the boat slowed the shark slowed too. Whatever the speed of the PT, the shark seemed to stay exactly the same distance in front of the prow until at last it tired of the game and swam off to spoil some poor fish's afternoon.

As at Tulagi, PT 109 was moored in the bushes at the Russells. The men built a catwalk out from the shore and draped canvas on overhanging limbs to catch rainwater and shelter the deck, where they slept on mattresses.

Because of the back condition that had troubled him since Harvard days, Kennedy found it more comfortable when he was on the boat to sleep on a plywood board, which he kept handy for that purpose. Occasionally he would allude to his back, but he said it was getting better. At times when he was not using the board the men often appropriated it to wash their clothes on. More than once it happened that when Kennedy was ready to turn in, the board was not where it was supposed to be, and this led to ribbing between skipper and crew.

"Mac, where's my board?" Kennedy asked Maguire one evening.

"What board?"

"You know what board."

"I hope that wasn't the board that Kowal was making cribbage sets out of and selling them."

"You've got two minutes to get the sets all back and glue them together," Kennedy declared.

Someone in the crew was always "riding" someone else, it seemed. For example, Drewitch rode Mauer. Or did, that is, until one afternoon a pistol shot rang out in the charthouse below the cockpit.

Mauer and Drewitch and one or two others were below shooting the breeze when Mauer decided it was time for him to clean his Colt .45. (PT sailors wore sidearms.) He sat on the chart table, snapped the clip out of his pistol and put a drop of oil on a rag. Drewitch found some better use for his time and started up the ladder to the deck. Mauer pulled back the slide of his pistol to eject the bullet he supposed was in the chamber. However, no bullet popped out, so, concluding that the chamber was empty, he let the slide slam forward. In the small charthouse the effect was like the blast of a Long Tom. Everyone in the room was stunned. There had been a bullet in the chamber, which for some reason had stuck when the ejector mechanism was operated. When the pistol fired, the bullet hit the aluminum handrail of the ladder Drewitch had just ascended.

"Mauer's out to get you, Drewitch," Maguire called when he had recovered his power of speech. "You'd better lay off him!"

Maguire sensed afterward that Drewitch *did* let up on Mauer, although Drewitch was not to be around much longer. Fate had in store for him the role of the Kennedy crew's first casualty in action.

ONE WELCOME INSTALLATION at the Russells base that Tulagi had lacked was a dock where the PT boats could refuel without the back-breaking work of hauling drums aboard and pumping 100-octane gasoline into the tanks through chamois strainers.

When the boats returned from patrol at dawn they would pull up to the dock and refuel through hoses. The standing orders were, however, that the crews had to refuel before they could knock off for breakfast and a few hours' sleep. Since it took a couple of hours to refuel all the boats on a patrol, the crew that filled up first would have a longer rest. Naturally, this led to intense competition to get to the head of the line. When they were released from patrol, the PTs would come thundering into the cove in a fierce race for the dock, an old wooden affair standing on coconut logs, with a large tool shed at one end.

As the days passed it was remarked that no crew got more rest than the crew of PT 109. From the time he had taken command nearly two months before Kennedy was possessed with a desire to make the boat go faster. He was forever instructing the motormacs, "Let's get more speed." He loved to be at the wheel, and he loved speed. On these sprints to the fuel dock he would roar into the cove with a rooster tail arching in his wake and throttles wide open. He would hold his speed to the last second, then order the engines into reverse just in time to brake his momentum in front of the dock.

The hairbreadth finishes began to worry the motormacs. The braking at such speed put a heavy strain on the engines. Drawdy cautioned Kennedy that the engines might not always reverse under such pressure. However, they always *had*, and Kennedy liked to win.

One morning when the clouds above the eastern horizon were pink and the palms on the shore mirrored in the glassy calm, he found himself in a furious race with another boat. Rather than fight for the lead all the way he decided to swing in behind the other boat and ride her wake. In this order the two boats went skimming across the water until the final stretch before the dock. Then Kennedy edged his throttles forward and swung back out again to challenge for the lead.

Gradually he crept up even with the other PT, and as they raced prow to prow the issue resolved itself into the simple matter of which skipper would have the nerve to hold his speed the longer with the dock rushing in on both of them. In the end Kennedy held just long enough to go in front.

Immediately he ordered the engines into reverse. All three conked out, and PT 109 went streaking at the dock like an eighty-foot missile on the loose.

On the dock, the fueling crew had reported and a work party under a warrant officer had entered the shed to get out the tools when the whole world came crashing down on them.

Tools flew in all directions. Wrenches, jacks, screwdrivers and hammers plopped into the water. Some of the men who were still outside toppled off the dock. Those on the inside who weren't too terrified to move clawed their way out. When they burst through the door, however, they beheld not the expected formation of Japanese dive bombers overhead, but a single PT boat sliced into a corner of the dock, her skinny bronzed skipper standing in his motionless cockpit, ruefully surveying the scene. Some of his crew were motionless, too, having been knocked flat by the crash.

The warrant officer howled at Lt. Kennedy, who was his senior. Shaken-up enlisted men stamped about the dock cussing out 109 and everyone aboard. A gale of indignation was blowing, and beyond uttering a word of quiet apology here and there, Kennedy could do little but wait for the storm to blow itself out. Unostentatiously, he tried backing the boat out, but this only made matters worse as more tools fell onto his deck and into the water.

The whole business might have had more serious consequences for Kennedy if Irish luck had not come to his rescue. At the height of the commotion two or three other PT boats were discovered to have broken away from their moorings. The attention of everyone ashore shifted to this greater emergency and Kennedy idled 109 away from the dock into a small stream where he moored out of sight until the trouble blew over. For some days afterward the crew referred to him as "Crash" Kennedy.

PATROL DUTY in the Russells was as uneventful as it had been in Tulagi. But before long, more serious matters were engaging their attention.

Within Admiral William F. Halsey's Third Fleet, a powerful amphibious armada was being formed under the designation of Task Force 31, commanded by Rear Admiral Richmond Kelly Turner, for the invasion of the New Georgia group. Its convoys were gathering with troops packed into the *President Jackson*, the *President Adams* and the *President Hayes*.

The destroyers *Talbot*, *Zane*, *Dent*, *Waters*, *Farenholt*, *Buchanan* and *McCalla*, among others, were screening the transports, LSTs, tugs and barges that made up Task Force 31. As part of TF 31 also, the New Georgia Motor Torpedo Boat Squadron was organized under Robert B. Kelly, of Philippines fame, who was now a lieutenant commander. A reserve unit remained under

Commander Calvert, while still a third unit called the Russell Islands Motor Torpedo Boat Squadron was commanded by Lt. Cluster. Its twelve boats included PT 109.

As had been contemplated before Kennedy left Tulagi, 109 returned briefly to Sesape in mid-June to have her three engines replaced with engines rebuilt at shops in the New Hebrides. After the refitting Kennedy was given an errand to do in Guadalcanal. Setting out, he asked Mauer to try his hand at plotting a course. Every member of a PT crew was supposed to know how to execute each function performed on the boat in case the man who did a particular job was disabled.

"I'd like to have our earliest time of arrival at Lunga," Kennedy said.

Mauer went down to the charthouse and after struggling with the unfamiliar problem for some time returned to the cockpit with his report.

"We'll be there about two o'clock, skipper," he said.

"About!" Kennedy exclaimed. "I don't want any *about*. I want to know what's the earliest time we can get there."

Mauer trudged back to the charthouse and tried again.

"Two-ten," he reported. The estimate proved correct.

"Good man," Kennedy complimented him, and Mauer felt well pleased with himself.

From Guadalcanal 109 returned to the Russells for the final preparations for the invasion.

Following preliminary landings on New Georgia by units of the 4th Marine Raider Battalion and the 103rd Infantry and heavy air raids on the Munda airstrip, the massive invasion fleet sailed across the Solomon Sea. On D-Day, June 30, the most important of several landings was made on the north coast of Rendova, where Commander Kelly proceeded to set up a base for the PT operations in the New Georgia campaign.

PT 109's mission in the hours of darkness preceding the landings was to patrol an area between the Russells and New

Georgia, with her torpedoes ready to help defend the convoys from any attacks on the flanks.

Kennedy's patrol was uneventful except that during the night the weather became increasingly dirty. By morning the gray sea was buffeting the PT boats brutally. On deck it was a feat to stand up without holding onto a ventilator or gun mount. Men off watch staggered below to lie on their bunks to guard against broken limbs. Even in bed they were tossed around like sacks. Drewitch, who had climbed into a lower bunk, had the greatest difficulty in staying in bed at all.

PT 109's orders were to return to the Russells upon the completion of the patrol, and she was making her way back tortuously when an accompanying boat sent up a distress signal. Kennedy shoved his three throttles forward and turned his wheel toward the stricken boat. The thought crossed his mind that this was a fine time for an eighty-foot boat with a plywood hull to develop trouble at sea. After laboring up mountains and plunging down valleys he finally reached the other boat to find that the savage waves had knocked a large patch off her hull. She was taking on water, although a mattress stuffed into the hole was averting disaster for the time being.

Above the wind the skipper of the boat hollered to Kennedy that he badly needed a bilge pump. There was none aboard 109, but Kennedy yelled back that he would try to get one from a destroyer they could see coming back from New Georgia. Hanging onto the wheel almost as much to keep his footing as to steer, he set off over the waves again and made it to the destroyer, whose captain ordered a pump brought up for transfer to 109.

As the two drew together the destroyer would rise high above PT 109. Then the destroyer would slide down a trough and 109 would soar above it. The two skippers had to maneuver with care to keep the vessels from slamming together lest the destroyer's steel hull crush the plywood shell of 109. Precariously the heavy one-cylinder pump was passed as if between two men on a teeter-totter.

Kennedy edged away from the destroyer and was circling back to the damaged boat when the top of a wave smote his port hull with such force that it jolted one of the torpedoes out of its tube. The torpedo banged into a heavy depth charge, a collision that brought together enough explosives to have blown Kennedy and his crew to bits, had not the two weapons been set to fire under different conditions. However, the depth charge toppled off its perch, crashed through the deck into the crew's quarters and landed on the bunk above where Drewitch was trying to sleep.

When Drewitch scrambled up, the violent rocking of the boat flung him across the room on his face, mashing his nose against his cheek and breaking two upper front teeth. Struggling to his feet, he half dove through the hatch and fell again. This time the crash split his right knee cap. Seeing him bleeding and in pain, Kennedy wanted to give him a shot of morphine, but Drewitch preferred to go without it. Kennedy got the pump to the other boat without further accident and stood by until a tender came to the rescue.

Arriving back in the Russells, he was conscious of the approving stares at the large hole punched in 109's deck by the fallen depth charge. It amused him that sailors on the ships that had not yet sailed were doubtless thinking that 109 must gallantly have come through a fight with Japanese planes or destroyers in the invasion.

Drewitch was removed to the hospital, and though he did not suspect it then, this was the end of 109 for him. He was to serve under Kennedy again, but on a different boat and in different circumstances.

By this time two more members had been added to the crew, both of them motormacs and both older than any of the others.

William Johnston at thirty-three had been in the South
Pacific for a long time and was more than fed up with it.
Expecting to be rotated home, he was assigned to 109 instead,
and the thought of going into another campaign on a PT boat
did little to brighten his spirits. Born in Dumbarton, Scotland,
he was two years old when his father, a plasterer, moved the
family to Dorchester, near Boston. Growing up, young Johnston used to hear his mother relate how on the trip from
Southampton they had seen the *Titanic* passing on her way to
doom. Before the war Johnston drove a trailer for the Gulf Oil
Company. He was attending a union meeting when the news
of the bombing of Pearl Harbor arrived. That week he had his
teeth filled and joined the Navy.

The second member was Patrick McMahon, whom the
crew came to call "Pop" or "Pappy" because he was, at
thirty-seven, their patriarch. Of all the members of the crew of
PT 109 who lived through the ordeal that lay ahead, Pappy
McMahon was to suffer the most and, in his stoical way, prove
to be the most uncomplaining. This son of a farmer was born at
Wyanet, Illinois. From boyhood he was fascinated by engines,
and in the twenties he worked as a mechanic for racing drivers
at dirt tracks in Southern California. At the time of Pearl Harbor he was a mechanic for the Detroit Street Railway Company. His stepson was serving as a submariner in the Navy. It
did not seem right to McMahon that the younger man should
be risking his life for the country while he stayed home, so
despite difficulty with the eye test, he enlisted in the Navy to,
in his words, "do some fighting or fixing." He had never been
on a boat larger than a ferry. He couldn't swim, and when he
was ordered to dive into a pool at boot training in San Diego,
he went to the bottom and had to be pulled out. He attended
a Navy Diesel school at the University of Missouri and volunteered for the PTs because he thought his mechanic's skill might
be useful on a small boat.

PT 109 had to be laid up again briefly for repair of the damage from the fallen depth charge. Shortly after the work was completed Kennedy received orders in mid-July to proceed to the forward operating base for motor torpedo boats at Rendova, one of the large islands in the Solomons, in the middle of the main battle then being fought in the Pacific.

"On your way, small fry," a destroyer blinked as 109 churned away from the Russells.

FIVE

RENDOVA HARBOR is a body of calm blue water roughly a mile wide and two miles long, formed by Rendova proper and a line of lesser islands festooned across its northern tip. On the south the harbor is sealed off by a mountain wall of jungle on Rendova. To the northwest the harbor looks out across reefs to the Solomon Sea. On the east and northeast it is enclosed by the lesser islands, small oblongs and circles of coconut palms bursting like sky rockets above dense foliage. Outside these islands flows Blanche Channel, the main axis of the waterways in this immediate vicinity of the Solomons. Across it lies New Georgia, where soldiers and Marines were then fighting a cruel battle to wrest the Munda airstrip from the Japanese. It is five and a half miles from Munda to Rendova Harbor.

The harbor was a wilderness until the Navy moved in and set up various installations. At the southeast end the Navy built its main base on Rendova proper. At the opposite end, toward Munda, was the PT base on Lumberi, a five-hundred-yard-long, kidney-shaped island with a dense crown of palms. Across a narrow channel from it lies Bau Island, which was used as a subsidiary PT headquarters.

A narrow sandy beach curves around the eastern tip of Lumberi and there, beside a varu tree with yellow flowers, a small

jetty had been built for unloading cargo. Visible from the water
was a conspicuous sign:

TODD CITY

The sign was made by stringing eight white-painted oil-
drum heads with black letters on a high rope suspended
between two palm trees. It was a memorial to Leon E. Todd,
Jr., of Commander Kelly's Squadron 9, who was the first PT man
killed at Rendova. Todd City was the name by which Lumberi
Island was best known to the sailors who operated out of the
base.

Back from the beach behind a screen of broad-leaved napa
bushes and raqosobelama vine the brush had been cleared away
for the headquarters. In a square formed by four tall palms stood
the operations dugout with a foundation of sand-filled fuel
drums, a superstructure of sandbags and a pyramidal tent for a
roof. Inside were tables, chairs, typewriters, maps, an Army field
phone, radio and coding equipment. Nearby was a sick bay and
a mess tent with a supply of Army C and K rations and little
else.

Lister bags held the drinking-water supply obtained from
streams flowing down Rendova Peak and chlorinated. Scattered about the island were tents for the motormacs, torpedomen, carpenters, metalsmiths and radiomen who made up the
permanent base crew. Near the tents were foxholes and gun
emplacements dug into the sandy ground, which was strewn
with rotting coconut husks and dead palm fronds.

Small black lizards slithered over the mangrove roots. Little
land crabs lugged their shells through the coral waste. Black
flies buzzed everywhere, maddeningly.

It was mid-afternoon when PT 109 rumbled into Rendova
Harbor after the long run from the Russells. Kennedy followed
his compass and charts to Lumberi and reported to the new base

commander, Lt. Commander Thomas G. Warfield. He had replaced Commander Kelly, who had been sent around to open a motor torpedo boat base at Rice Anchorage on the far side of New Georgia. At this time also Admiral Turner had been replaced by Admiral Theodore S. Wilkinson as Commander, TF 31.

At Rendova the PT boats, now numbering between fifteen and twenty, were moored in "nests" of three to a buoy, with the buoys scattered about the harbor in the vicinity of Lumberi. Warfield assigned Kennedy to a buoy and introduced him to some of the other officers at the base.

Warfield was a strict officer. While he was a freshman at the University of Nebraska, Senator George Norris appointed him to the United States Naval Academy, where he caught his first glimpse of salt water. After graduation in 1932 he served on battleships and was in Manila on December 7 when the Japanese attacked. The *Marshal Joffre* had just arrived in port, and it was Warfield who was put in command with orders to sail the ship to Australia before the Japanese could sink or capture her. He had to keep an armed watch on the multi-lingual crew, dodge minefields and, on one occasion, prepare to scuttle when Japanese men-of-war appeared on the horizon. In spite of everything, however, he reached Darwin. Later he took the *Marshal Joffre* to San Francisco to be converted into the *Rochambeau*, while he went to Melville to be converted into a PT officer.

Among those to whom he introduced Kennedy at headquarters were Lt. Arthur H. Berndtson of Oakland, who was executive officer of the base, and Lt. James L. Woods of Houston, the communications officer. They talked a while about the problems of the PT skippers and their missions among the islands. Then Kennedy took his boat out and moored her to a buoy, but not for long.

In spite of their journey of some ten hours from the Russells, Lt. Kennedy and his crew were ordered out on patrol their first night at Rendova. From then on through the fateful events of August their destiny was to lie within an elongated triangle of coral reefs, islands and salt water, less than fifty miles in length, which in a happier time would have evoked the grandeur of Robert Louis Stevenson's

> Billows and breeze,
> Mountains and seas,
> Islands of rain and sun.

The triangle begins at Rendova Harbor and runs west through open sea to Vella Lavella Island. There it cuts northward across Vella Gulf to Kolombangara Island, a massive extinct volcano covered with jungle. Thence it turns south again across the western tip of New Georgia to Rendova. Lying entirely within this triangle are Gizo Island and its satellite islands; Blackett Strait, a deep body of water between Gizo and Kolombangara; and Ferguson Passage, which connects Blackett with the sea.

Roughly within the triangle also were the two focal points of Japanese resistance in the area, which affected all local military activity. One of these was the Munda airstrip, before which the Japanese were giving ground ditch by ditch. The other lay north of Munda, across Kula Gulf, on the eastern side of Kolombangara Island. There, at Vila Plantation, the enemy had an airstrip and base. If they were to have any hope of retaining a foothold in the Western Solomons now, the Japanese had to retain Vila, and they were making a desperate effort to do so.

From their great base at Rabaul they moved men and supplies at night down along New Georgia Sound, renowned among American airmen and sailors since Guadalcanal days as "the Slot." From the Slot reinforcements bound for Vila would turn south into Vella Gulf between Vella Lavella and Kolombangara and then through Blackett Strait to their destination. Generally

the men and supplies were carried on motorized barges, but frequently the Japanese would attempt a much heavier reinforce-
ment by organizing an "Express," consisting of several destroyers,
and ramming it through to Vila. It was from this base on Kolombangara that the Japanese forces at Munda were being supplied.

The principal mission of the PT boats operating out of Rendova Harbor was to intercept these nocturnal invasions of
Blackett Strait and thus starve out Vila.

After a run through the Solomon Sea from Rendova the PTs
would enter Blackett Strait through one of two passages. The
one nearer Rendova is Ferguson Passage, which cuts between
the Gizo Island reefs and the Wana Wana Island reefs, west of
New Georgia. The farther one is Gizo Strait, separating Gizo
and Vella Lavella.

THE FIRST NIGHT OUT of Rendova the islands and passages were
just lines on a map to Kennedy, who assiduously kept his division leader in sight as he patrolled through the unfamiliar
region. The men were alert and nervous. They knew the Japanese held many of the islands that could be seen dimly in the
night, but they did not know precisely which islands. Even the
names of the islands seemed weird, especially Gizo, which in the
native tongue means "plague." Each new turn, each dark lump
of land aroused fresh trepidation.

In their first penetration of enemy waters things that hith-
erto had been taken for granted now aroused deep anxieties. On
scores of cruises and patrols at Tulagi and the Russell Islands PT
109 had run zigzag courses. But now when Kennedy, following
the division leader, zigzagged, Pappy McMahon fretted at the
possibility that the engines would overheat.

In the middle of the night the leading boat suddenly opened
machine-gun fire on a dark shape against a distant shore, and
all the other boats, including 109, fired along the line of the

first boat's tracers. Some of the tracers seemed to ricochet off into the black, but there was no answering fire. The shape, if a shape was really there at all, vanished.

When the stars began to fade, the patrol turned about and returned to Rendova.

"This isn't so bad," McMahon observed.

Yet all were soon to learn that life at Rendova was drastically different from the easygoing staging days at Tulagi and the Russell Islands. For months war had seemed comfortably distant most of the time. Now the air was heavy with it. Uneasiness and fear lay just below the surface everywhere. Like an ocean current that cannot be seen, this fear conditioned the air above. Men became tense. With scuttlebutt about casualties passing endlessly among the boats, they wondered whether they would be wounded or killed. They speculated on how they would react under attack, sinking, capture. Longing for the old life at home grew keener. The memory of the good things about it dimmed memories of the bad. Men wondered when that life would be resumed and asked themselves whether, even with the best of luck, it would ever again be the same as it was.

The sights and sounds of war were all about them. From their boat Kennedy and his men could watch American planes bombing Munda. On the large raids the bombs falling from high-flying bombers looked in the distance like soot sifting down from a stovepipe that had been shaken. Frequently the PT crews could see muzzle flashes from the guns on Captain Arleigh A. ("Thirty-one Knot") Burke's destroyers, sweeping up Blanche Channel firing at Japanese shore batteries on New Georgia. Day and night American 155-millimeter guns on Rendova kept up a long-range bombardment of Munda. In their boats the PT men could hear the swoosh of shells passing overhead.

As the battle for Munda neared a climax, the Japanese went to frantic lengths to push men and supplies through Blackett Strait.

In the Solomons at that time the Allies themselves were sorely short of ships, particularly destroyers. Consequently, the Navy relied heavily on the PT boats to harass enemy movements at night in the narrow waters.

Every afternoon Warfield received radioed orders from Commander, TF 31, in Guadalcanal, to send patrols to the vicinity of Gizo, Kolombangara and Vella Lavella. At about four o'clock each day Warfield would summon the boat skippers, sending an LCVP around the harbor to pick up those who had not yet come in to Lumberi. When all were assembled at the operations dugout he held a briefing on the night's operations, at which time each skipper received his individual orders. It did not take Kennedy long to discover that the demands on the PTs were such that 109 would have to go out night after night, sometimes many nights in succession without rest.

Although the strain soon began to tell on officers and men alike, PT 109's early missions out of Rendova passed without serious mishap.

One night at sea Kennedy received word by radio that American B-25 bombers were attacking a Japanese warship north of Vella Lavella. He opened his engines wide and ripped up Blackett Strait into Vella Gulf. The crew could see aerial flares hanging low over the water and they reminded Harris of a row of lights along a waterfront street. Any place where flares were glowing was no place for a PT boat, which must rely on surprise for effectiveness and self-defense. Also the engagement was still sufficiently far away to take Kennedy beyond his range. He left the situation in the hands of the B-25s, therefore, and returned to his patrol station.

Another night 109 was patrolling well up in Vella Gulf. Kennedy had ordered two of the engines shut off and was idling on the third. This was standard operating procedure for the PTs when they had reached their stations and were patrolling a given area. The powerful engines produced a very heavy wake. Seen from the air it could lead an enemy plane to a boat like a road map. One engine idling held the wake as well as the noise to a minimum.

By the early hours of the morning PT 109 was far from its base. The men were edgy. Above the rumble of the engine and the burbling exhaust they could hear nothing. In all directions it was pitch black. As starkly as on the Day of Judgment, an incandescent yellowish light burst directly overhead and hung in the sky illuminating every last detail of the boat and every line of the upturned faces of the men aboard. Their fear was almost paralyzing. Some of the men believed they were about to be killed.

Harris was on watch in the stern, standing strapped to the 20-millimeter anti-aircraft gun. He was wearing a helmet above his dark, nervous eyes and a kapok life jacket bulged under his chin. In the air off the starboard bow he caught sight of the tail of a plane flying away. He yanked the gun around and fired ahead of it. The shot missed. He fired again and missed again. He was firing steadily when he heard the piercing voice of Kennedy shouting, "Knock it off, Harris!"

The skipper came tearing down the deck.

"Knock it off, knock it off," he was shouting. "It's a Black Cat."

Harris ceased firing. "Black Cat" was the nickname of the American PBY Catalina patrol planes. The pilot had spotted the boat in the dark and dropped the flare to identify her. Recognizing the PT, he was resuming his own patrol when Harris opened fire. Fortunately, the pilot was able to identify himself on the radio to Maguire in time for Kennedy to call Harris off before he found the target.

Planes were the bane of the PT boats. Generally, a PT skipper could not tell whether an aircraft approaching in the dark (if he was aware of it at all above the noise of his own engines) was friend or foe. The pilot above had the same difficulty. Consequently the PTs operating out of Rendova were suffering severe casualties from American planes and in turn were inflicting casualties on American pilots.

After dawn on July 20 PT 164, PT 166 and PT 168 had just emerged from Ferguson Passage on their way back to Rendova when four Army B-25s descended on them. One of the boats had been damaged in a collision with a log. The two others reduced their speed to stay with her. Thus the three were still at sea at an hour when the B-25 crews, returning to Henderson Field from a night mission, had been told that no friendly vessels would be in the area. The PT crews were unconcerned by the approaching bombers until the machine guns on the leading plane ripped an ugly path through the water toward them. The men tried frantically to identify themselves by radio, semaphore and Very pistol, but the bombers roared in on a strafing run. Without orders gunners on PT 164 and PT 166 returned the fire. In the blazing skirmish that ensued, PT 166 caught fire. The crew, some of them severely wounded, jumped overboard seconds before the boat exploded and sank.

One of the PT gunners got to the heart of a B-25. Trailing smoke, the bomber cartwheeled across the sky and crashed into the sea five miles away. PT 168 was afire, but the crew extinguished the flames. With Lt. Edward Macauley 3rd at the wheel, 168 sped to the fallen plane. The PT crew was in a rage at the crew of the B-25, but the spectacle at the scene of the crash gave them something else to think about. The bomber pilot and two of his crew were dead. Three others were injured. These three and eleven wounded sailors rode back to Rendova in awful silence.

In view of these tragic misreckonings Kennedy was most uneasy one night off Gizo when two planes which he was able to identify as PBYs began making runs in turn over PT 109. As one of them was passing over he turned to Maguire, who, as the radioman, was always standing at his right hand in the cockpit, and he said, "Ask that guy what's going on up there."

There was an explosion nearby.

"Tell him they nearly hit us," Kennedy shouted.

A confusing exchange of messages followed. One of the PBY pilots said he would call his partner off and leave. Then Maguire picked up a report that a Japanese float plane was in the area. These Zeros on pontoons were dreaded above all by the motor torpedo boat sailors. PT 109's predicament was simply too precarious for anyone aboard to tolerate.

"Tell them that we'll fire at the next plane that comes over us," Kennedy instructed Maguire.

"That broke up the party all right," Maguire recalled afterward.

The days and nights were beginning to take on such a sameness that the PT crews had difficulty distinguishing one twenty-four-hour period from another.

In the evenings sailors whose boats were to remain moored in Rendova Harbor for the night would stand on deck and mock and cheer sailors on the boats that were heading out on patrol. "Give 'em hell there, boy," someone would yell. This would set off an exchange of razzing back and forth across the water, with the outbound sailors thumbing their noses at those securely tied to the buoys.

The nerves of men going out tightened as they neared Ferguson Passage. By this time all of them knew that beyond Ferguson they would be in water surrounded by Japanese. The enemy would be on all sides of them—on Gizo, on Vella Lavella, on Kolombangara, on New Georgia.

Nights degenerated into a disturbing mixture of dozing while off duty, or standing tensely on deck, or leaping up in alarm at the cry of "General quarters," as the horizon flashed with tracers or a cloud came aglow with the garish light of a flare or an unidentified shadow moved to starboard or port.

Brief moments of danger and excitement were woven with splashes of brilliance into long hours of dark monotony. So far as

Kennedy and the men of 109 were concerned at least, no action ever seemed to be decisive.

The typical PT night patrol was an almost absurdly intangible form of warfare. The operation was conducted on dark waters against black outlines of islands. Barges deliberately moved close to the islands and when fired upon ducked up a stream or successfully sought invisibility beneath overhanging trees. They seldom appeared to PT skippers as more than vague shapes in the distance. At one moment a skipper would see a shape, then he would not see a shape and in the end he would not be sure a shape had been there at all. Sometimes he fired at a real barge; at other times he tore the night apart shooting at shadows. The very uncertainty of what lurked ahead in the dark strained the nerves, and rarely did a skipper enjoy any great satisfaction of triumph because the effect of his bullets on the target was seldom known. On top of all the other difficulties there was the hazard that the distant shape might be another PT boat.

When at last the first pale glow of dawn would awaken beyond Wana Wana, the boats would be heading back to the base again. The men would feel comparatively safe once more, and when they nosed past Lumberi to welcoming cheers from the beach their spirits would soar. Then as the day, so similar to the one before, wore on and thoughts of approaching night drowned the exuberance of the sunrise, men would grow serious again. Tension would begin to rise, and they would feel heavy and tired.

Life on the boats was becoming miserable. The men had turned yellowish from atabrine taken to suppress malaria. Dysentery was draining their strength and stamina. Some of them could tell they were getting thin by the way their wrist watches slid up and down their arms. There was nothing cold to drink, and all became disgusted with the heavy doses of chlorine in the warm drinking water. Officers and men were eating out of cans, mostly Spam. One of the men reported to Kennedy that another boat had received a ration of bread from an Army bakery. Kennedy took off in a small boat, and when he returned, everyone's spirits were raised by a few slices of fresh bread for the first time in days.

By midday the sun was a pot-bellied stove. There was no shade on the water and the crew's quarters would get so hot and airless that clothing felt intolerably uncomfortable. Dress degenerated to a point where men started coming to meals with no clothes on at all. Kennedy promptly put a stop to this. He made a rule that no one could come to the table without at least a pair of undershorts, or skivvies, on.

Sleeping below was unbearable. The quarters had become foul-smelling. The mattresses had no covers left, and when anyone lay on a mattress for any length of time it became soaked with sweat. In spite of the burning sun men preferred to sleep on the deck. Kennedy used to sleep next to a torpedo tube or sometimes on the plywood canopy of the day room. The men found that sleeping in this heat produced stupor, and no one could sleep very long anyhow. Eyes burned from a sleeplessness that caused irritability over trifles that would have been laughed off before. At night at sea men were too taut to sleep well even when they had some time off watch to lie on the deck. Then back at the base in the mornings they would have to haul gasoline drums up planks with ropes from Higgins boats and refuel before they could relax for a few hours. Frequently an air raid made them heave the drums overboard and then they would have to start all over again.

In the afternoons the work of getting ready for patrol would have to be resumed. Guns had to be cleaned, ammunition stored, torpedoes and radio checked, engines oiled. Working down in the engine room was the worst ordeal of all. The temperature seemed to be up around 110 degrees most of the time. The motormacs went about forever hot, sticky and spattered with grease.

Often toward late afternoon rain clouds would roll down the slope of Rendova Peak, and a heavy tropical shower would splash across the flat surface of the harbor, bringing momentary relief. Then the sun would shine through, sometimes throwing a magnificent rainbow across a channel like a high bridge with each end anchored to an island. But on the boat the hull would trap the humidity and hold it in the charthouse and day room and sleeping quarters just as the mangroves and napa bushes on Lumberi held the warm dampness around the musty tents under the ceiling of palms.

Sometimes men would try swimming off PT 109, but only when someone was standing guard on deck with a rifle. Sharks infest the Solomons,[†] and the thought of them took the zest out of swimming.

As evening approached there would be a pause. A phonograph would be turned on. Some of the sailors would try napping on deck. Others would write letters. This was particularly true of those who expected that their boat would be going out on that night's patrol. Men who would have to spend another night on the black waters before the sun would rise again were likely to be the first to reach for V-mail. On 109 Mauer would descend to the galley and turn up the hotplate. Then it would be time for Kennedy to return from the briefing with his orders for the night. If 109 was going out, the men would solemnly get ready to shove off some time after 6 P.M.

Late in the afternoon of July 19 the skipper came aboard with word that they would be going up to Blackett Strait to patrol off Gizo again. When a few hours later they arrived at their station it was dark as usual, but the clouds were luminous and hung very low over the water. Together with another boat some dis-

---

[†]On an expedition that Elliott Erwitt, the photographer, and I made to the Solomons in preparing this book, Erwitt saw a shark just off Lumberi while taking a photograph. On the beach we found the skull of a whale.

tance out on her port beam PT 109 idled back and forth on station between Gizo and Kolombangara. Hours passed and nothing happened to indicate that this night would be different from any of the preceding nights.

Kennedy was standing in the cockpit at the wheel. Radioman Maguire, as usual, was standing at his right side. Harris had his fists clenched on the machine guns in the forward gun turret. Mauer was on deck leaning against the quartermaster's locker. Johnston, off watch, was lying on the deck near the ladder leading down into the engine room. Drawdy was on the ladder, half in and half out of the hatch in a position to drop quickly into the engine room if he were needed by McMahon, who was on duty there. Drawdy was leaning with his head and chest above the deck talking with Kowal, who was above him in the after gun turret on the port side, facing the stern.

With his gaze upturned toward Kowal, Drawdy saw an airplane appear on the port side at an altitude that looked to be less than a hundred feet. The night clouds reflected enough light for him to see the Rising Sun on the wings.

He shouted hoarsely to Ensign Thom, who was making his way forward to speak to Kennedy. At that instant there was a tremendous "Boom! Boom!" Two bright orange flashes burst off the port beam between 109 and the other boat. PT 109 was rocked violently to starboard.

Kowal felt a pain in his scalp. Drawdy was blown clear out of the hatch, and his head crashed against the deck. His scalp pained too.

Fragments in the form of Ford car door handles, safety razors, faucets and other scrap that Japan had been importing from the United States for years before the war, sliced into 109 and her rigging from bow to stern. Bulkheads were pierced. One large chunk of iron smashed clear through the boat from port to starboard, leaving a large hole above the waterline on the starboard side. A glowing-hot fragment almost simultaneously severed a gas line and welded it together again.

The engine on which the boat was idling stalled. McMahon was frightened. If the engines should fail under an air attack, 109 would be an easy target. In a moment, however, he had all three engines running. Kennedy jammed the three throttles forward, swung his wheel to port and raced along a circle away from the plane's course.

Kowal removed his helmet and ran his hand along his head. He discovered that his hair was standing on end, and he realized that the ache was coming from the nervous tightening of his scalp. He was relieved to think he had not been hit, and turned his attention back to the guns.

Drawdy, sprawled on deck, appeared to be worse off. Maguire jumped from the cockpit and asked, "Were you hit?"

"My head," he replied. Drawdy took off his helmet and blood started to trickle down his forehead.

Maguire helped him down to the charthouse and with the aid of Mauer wiped away the blood to dress the wound. Once the blood had been removed, however, they could find no wound in Drawdy's head. While they were looking for it, Drawdy himself discovered that his left arm and hand were bleeding. Slivers of shrapnel were stuck in his arm, and the middle finger was sliced. When he had removed his helmet on deck, the blood from his hand had dripped to his head. Because his head hurt from the blow of the fall, he assumed the blood was flowing from a scalp wound.

Up in the after gun turret, Kowal, his headache gone, was experiencing a strange sensation. He was high and dry, but his right foot was getting wet. At first he paid no attention to it but presently, his right shoe began to squish whenever he stepped on it. This worried him, and he went down to the charthouse. In the dim blue light Mauer removed the shoe. It was half full of blood. Only then did Kowal discover a jagged piece of shrapnel sticking painlessly into his leg above the ankle.

Thus PT 109's first casualties inflicted by the enemy, thought to be head injuries, turned out to be a wounded arm and a wounded leg.

Kennedy decided that neither Kowal nor Drawdy was wounded seriously enough to warrant returning to Rendova, and the patrol continued through the night.

Entering the harbor at daybreak, the men made a couple of discoveries that testified to their good luck. For one thing, shrapnel piercing the hull had gashed the ladder on which Drawdy had been standing. Somehow the concussion of the bombs had blown him out of the hatch in time to save his body from being mangled. For another, an ugly dent had been bashed in the metal splinter shield that ran, about head high, along the port side of the cockpit beside the wheel.

If the shield had not been there or if it had not been strong enough to withstand the force of the shrapnel, it was all too likely that PT 109 would have returned to Rendova that morning minus a live skipper.

"This is about the limit for you," Mauer told Kennedy.

"What about yourself?" Kennedy answered, pointing to a hole in the quartermaster's locker.

These were signs of good luck, to be sure, but the bombing represented a change of luck for the worse for 109. She had been hit in many places. Her galley had been pierced. A patch more than twelve inches square had to be placed above the waterline on the starboard side.

Worse still, the enemy had drawn blood. Kowal and Drawdy had to be sent back to the hospital at Tulagi. They would never see PT 109 again. Along with Drewitch, however, they would be serving with Lt. Kennedy again in another boat under different hazards.

A further omen appeared on the night of July 30 when PT

109 along with seven other boats was dispatched to deal with an expected invasion of Japanese shipping in Blackett Strait. On the way to her station west of Makuti Island, which lies just inside Ferguson Passage, PT 109 developed rudder trouble, and Kennedy had to return to Rendova for repairs.

Conditions on the boats were now the worst ever. The crew had not had any fresh food in a week when Kennedy learned that a group of LCTs was shuttling supplies ashore on New Georgia five miles below Munda. He took a quick run down Blanche Channel, boarded the command ship, LCT 161, and begged five pounds of New Zealand mutton off the ship's cook and the commanding officer, Lt. (jg) Pickett Lumpkin, who recognized Kennedy as the Ambassador's son. Lumpkin recalled sadly that he had been in Boston exactly a year before and Kennedy promised that if the two of them ever saw Boston again he would buy Lumpkin a lobster dinner in return for the New Zealand mutton.

He returned to Rendova with the last booty he was ever to beg or borrow for PT 109.

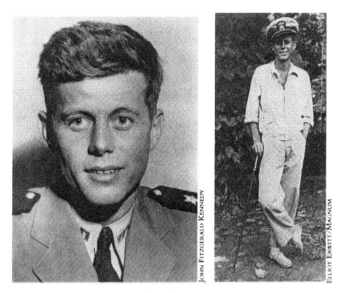

Lt. John F. Kennedy (left). A lighter moment: Lt. Kennedy in the Solomons (right).

Lt. Kennedy at the wheel of PT 109.

John F. Kennedy (above
right, standing) and his
PT crew "somewhere in
the South Pacific" in
early July, 1943.

PT boats underway for friendly craft identification photo taken on
October 8, 1943. PT 59 is in foreground and PT 48 is in center.

A PT boat at speed.

The *Amagiri*—the Japanese destroyer that rammed
and sank PT 109 on August 2, 1943.

On board the *Amagiri* shortly before the night
of the collision, Commander Hanami (far right)
and Captain Yamashiro (without hat) listen to
a band concert while the ship is undergoing
repairs at Rabaul.

Captain Yamashiro,
commander of 11th
Destroyer Flotilla
and senior officer on
board the *Amagiri* on the
night of the collision
with PT 109.

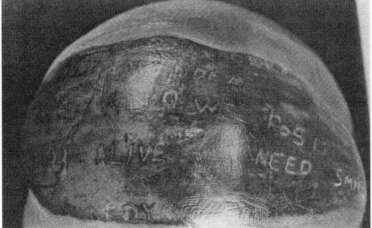

The quarter of a coconut shell with Lt. Kennedy's message on it,
which later sat on his desk at the White House.

The Tulagi PT boat base, named for Cdr. Allen P. Calvert, circa 1943.

Lt. John F. Kennedy is presented with Navy and Marine Corps Medal by Captain Frederick L. Conklin, U.S.N., in 1945.

Football at Hyannis Port reunion in the fall of 1944. Left to right: George Ross, Leonard J. Thom, James A. Reed, Paul Fay (later Under Secretary of the Navy in the Kennedy administration) and John F. Kennedy.

President Kennedy, with a model, shows the author (out of photo on left) his position at the wheel at the moment of collision, whence he was hurled back against the rear of the cockpit, injuring his back.

SIX

IT WAS NOON on August 1, a clear, hot day. Snow-white cumulus clouds billowed over the deep blue South Pacific for thousands of miles.

The Japanese destroyers *Amagiri*, *Hagikaze*, *Arashi* and *Shigure* were at sea north of Bougainville. They were steaming to Vila, the base on Kolombangara, where they were due at midnight to put ashore nine hundred soldiers and more than seventy tons of supplies to reinforce the defenders of Munda.

The flagship *Hagikaze* and the *Arashi* and *Shigure*, each packed with three hundred soldiers, stood in line heading southward. The *Amagiri* hovered about them as an escort, moving up and down the column, sometimes on one side, sometimes on the other. Occasionally she would steam ahead of the *Hagikaze*, scanning the horizon, then drop to the rear of the line, her depth charges ready in case any American submarines should come in.

The *Amagiri* was a new gray two-stacker carrying thirteen officers and two hundred and forty-five men under thirty-four-year-old Lt. Commander Kohei Hanami, a stocky, muscular man with an intelligent square face and close-cropped hair. He had graduated from the Naval Academy at Etajima, Japan's equivalent of Annapolis, in 1928. He was a serious officer who paid strict attention to his responsibilities. Off duty, he was polite and genial. When the war began he was command-ing the destroyer *Asanagi* in the Marshall Islands. He took part in the invasion of the Gilbert Islands, Wake Island and New Britain. In September 1942 he became skipper of the destroyer *Akebono* and in June 1943 was put in command of the *Amagiri* at Rabaul.

It was from this wide blue harbor, ringed with mountains and extinct volcanoes, that the four destroyers had put to sea some hours earlier. In the battle of Kula Gulf on July 6, the action in which the American cruiser *Helena* was sunk, the *Amagiri* had taken four hits, and her forward radio room and electrical cir-cuits had just been repaired in time for her to join the "Express" to Vila.

Rabaul was the main base of supplies for all Japanese forces in New Guinea and the Solomons, and in the summer of 1943 it was a place of frantic activity. Since June the American air raids had been coming with increasing ferocity. Now and then between attacks base personnel could get in a game of volley ball, but officers and men of the ships in port would have to remain aboard all the time to be ready to get under way at the approach of bombers. While the *Amagiri* was laid up a Navy band came aboard and gave a concert on deck.

Not only was the Japanese position in the Solomons by now desperate, but in the face of American planes and warships it was becoming extremely difficult to get men and supplies through to improve the situation. It was one of these supply missions down the Slot to Vila that had resulted in the battle of Kula Gulf. And a fortnight later the destroyers *Yugure* and *Kiyonami* were bombed and sunk by American planes while convoying in the Slot south of Choiseul Island.

Then on July 21 the destroyer *Ariake* and two accompanying vessels slipped through to Vila by an alternate route. Instead of continuing down the Slot along the north side of Kolombangara and moving into Vila through Kula Gulf, they remained in the

Slot only as far as Vella Lavella. There they swung into Vella Gulf and passed south of Kolombangara through Blackett Strait and thence to Vila.

The fact that these three ships had been able to traverse this route unmolested encouraged the Japanese to try a greater effort through Blackett Strait. Therefore, on July 29 the commanding officers of the *Amagiri*, *Hagikaze*, *Arashi* and *Shigure* received a summons from Vice-Admiral Tomoshige Samejima to an immediate conference aboard the *Hagikaze*.

At this meeting the four destroyer captains were given orders to form a convoy and steam through Blackett Strait after dark on August 1, a night chosen because it would be moonless.

Within hours cases of bullets and shells, a small amount of meat, tons of canned food and sacks of rice were being loaded aboard the *Hagikaze*, *Arashi* and *Shigure*. All was going well enough until the Army began trucking large quantities of beer and sake to the piers as part of the rations of the nine hundred troops. The Navy demurred. The Army insisted. The Navy said that with all the other cargo the destroyers would not have space for beer and wine. The Army said that the spirits would be needed to inspire banzai charges on New Georgia. After a long wrangle a compromise was reached. About half the bottles were put aboard.

Finally, the troops filed aboard the *Hagikaze*, *Arashi* and *Shigure*. They were fully equipped for combat and carried their own individual rations, which were meager. In the heat there was considerable jockeying among the soldiers for places on deck. No one wanted to be stuck in the crowded, stifling quarters below.

The unbearable loss of destroyers that the Japanese were experiencing created deep pessimism among the officers and men who sailed them. As the four ships rounded Bougainville at noon that day it was rather commonly supposed aboard that one of them would not return. In fact the skipper of the *Shigure*,

Lt. Commander Tameichi Hara, had left all his personal effects in a trunk with a friend at Rabaul and had asked that the trunk be shipped home if he did not come back.

THAT SAME NOON it was quiet in Rendova Harbor. There was even a lull in the long-range bombardment of Munda by the 155-millimeters. On most of the PT boats the work of refueling was over by this time, but gunner's mates were still delving through layers of monotony oiling their machine guns and stacking ammunition for the anti-aircraft guns on the stern. Somewhere below deck a phonograph was asking, "Pardon me, boy, is that the Chattanooga Choo-choo . . . ?"

PT 164 had just arrived from Tulagi with a load of spare parts, which its crew was preparing to unload. The squadrons had run seriously low on extra propellers, carburetors, magneto points, gaskets, armatures and other parts that were included in the shipment. If the new boat had brought a cargo of steaks, it could not have been more welcome.

The only other boat on which anything unusual appeared to be happening was PT 109, where the men were preparing for a small experiment in weaponry. Someone had got the idea that a powerful gun on the foredeck would make the plywood boat a better match for the steel barges of the Japanese. It was decided, therefore, to install an old Army 37-millimeter anti-tank gun on the foredeck of PT 109 to test its effectiveness in 109's next engagement with a barge.

Around noon the crew saw Kennedy approaching with the gun in a Higgins boat, and Maguire remarked that if any weapon was available that a PT could carry, the skipper would be the one to take it.

Most of the men were in a good mood because PT 109, having been out on patrol for several nights in succession, was due at last to spend the night of August 1–2 at Rendova.

When the Higgins boat came alongside, they hauled the anti-tank gun and a couple of two-by-eight planks aboard. They laid the two planks along either side of the foredeck. Then they lifted the gun, the wheels of which had been removed, and placed it in position with its axles resting on the planks. After that they waited for some carpenters to come out from Lumberi to nail down the planks and bracket the axles to them.

The crew now contained a number of new faces. Ensign Thom, Harris, Maguire, Mauer, McMahon, Kirksey and Johnston were still aboard. But with Drewitch, Kowal and Drawdy in the hospital, Kennedy had had to get replacements.

One was Torpedoman 2/c Raymond Starkey of Garden Grove, California, a heavy-set, graying man of twenty-nine. His maternal grandfather had been a midshipman in the British Navy and had jumped ship in Canada, married a Canadian girl and moved his family by stages to the West. His forebears on his father's side came from the town of Starkey, in Yates County, New York. His great-great-grandfather fought with the Union Army at Gettysburg and was wounded. What with the depression and poor health in his youth, Ray Starkey had had a harsh life. After graduating from high school he worked as a commercial fisherman out of Newport Beach and other California ports and then got a job in the oil fields. When he enlisted in the Navy after Pearl Harbor he was married and had one child.

Starkey transferred to PT 109 because he could not abide his own skipper, whom he called an "Ivy League snob." When a base officer at Lumberi told him Kennedy needed a man, Starkey elected to switch to PT 109 on the assumption that at least it was likely to be the lesser of two evils. As a general rule Starkey was less than predisposed toward wealthy college graduates. "When I met Kennedy," he recalled afterward, "he gave me the impression of being the best type of college kid—all business, but a sense of humor and modest and considerate of enlisted men."

Motor Machinist's Mate 1/c Gerard E. Zinser took over Drawdy's post in the engine room. At twenty-five, he was 109's only career Navy man. He had grown up in Belleville, Illinois, and, like Starkey's, his family had suffered from the depression. After a couple of years in high school he worked in a Civilian Conservation Corps camp in northern Illinois. He joined the Navy in 1937 and took some pride in a bit of naval tradition in his family: his uncle had sailed in the U.S.S. *Monterey* in the Great White Fleet. During the late thirties, Zinser saw the world in the cruisers *Cincinnati* and *Trenton*. In 1941 he was assigned to PT boats, sent to the Packard plant in Detroit to familiarize himself with the engines and then transferred to a PT squadron at the Navy Yard in Brooklyn. On the afternoon of Sunday, December 7, while his wife, who was expecting the first of eight children, was preparing dinner, Zinser was in the living room of their apartment. He was listening to a professional football game between the New York Giants and the old Brooklyn Dodgers, when the broadcast was interrupted by a news flash. After he had heard it Zinser walked into the kitchen.

"Well, that's it," he said.

"Game over?" his wife inquired.

"The Japs have attacked Pearl Harbor," he replied.

"Will you have to go? How long will it last?" Mrs. Zinser asked, and then reasoned that both questions were foolish.

Another newcomer was Motor Machinist's Mate 2/c Harold W. Marney, who was assigned by Lt. Kennedy as a gunner in place of Kowal. Marney was a prankish youth of nineteen, whose chief interest in life was machinery. One of three children in the family, he was born in Chicopee, Massachusetts, but grew up in Springfield where his father was an inspector for Westinghouse. Young Marney went through the tenth grade at a trade school and enlisted in the Navy at seventeen, a month before Pearl Harbor.

The fourth new crew member was Seaman 2/c Raymond Albert of Akron. Albert was typical of thousands of cocky young sailors one used to see during the war in Times Square and San Francisco, shuffling along in blue blouse and white cap, with a girl on one arm, a fresh tattoo on the other and an air of restlessness. After eleven years of schooling he joined the Navy in Cleveland a few months after Pearl Harbor. Originally he was sent to radio school at Texas A & M, but later he volunteered for PT boats. He was twenty years old and a trifle brash.

ASHORE EARLY in the afternoon Lt. Woods sought out Commander Warfield. He told him that the Navy base radio station across the harbor on Rendova had received an important message for PT headquarters from Commander, TF 31, at Koli Point and that it was being relayed to Lumberi.

Shortly afterward a radioman handed the decoded message to Commander Warfield, who read it and raised his eyebrows. It was the most urgent and sweeping order issued to him since he had taken command of the PT base. This was the message:[†]

DATE/TIME GROUP 3 1 2 3 5 6

FROM: CTF 31

TO (ACTION) COMMTBRON (RENDOVA) APC 28:1 MAR RD REG:
TO (INFO): COMSOPAC CTG 31.2; ATFC SOPAC

MOST SECRET

INDICATIONS EXPRESS MAY RUN TONIGHT ONE DASH TWO
(1–2) AUGUST X ALSO HEAVY BARGE TRAFFIC TO BAIROKO OR
SUNDAY INLET X WARFIELD OPERATE MAXIMUM NUMBER

[†]The Xs stand for periods. "Love" denotes local time. Area Baker (B) refers to Blackett Strait.

PETER TARES (PT) IN AREA BAKER (B) X KELLY OPERATE ALL
AVAILABLE PETER TARES (PT) IN KULA GULF SOUTH OF LINE
BAMBARI DASH RICE X BURKE WITH SIX (6) DESTROYERS GOES
UP SLOT ARRIVING NORTH OF KOLOMBANGARA AT ZERO
ZERO THIRTY LOVE (0030L) AUGUST SECOND (2ND) X IF KELLYS
BOATS FORCED RETIRE TO LEVER DURING NIGHT ROUTE
THEM CLOSE IN NEW GEORGIA SHORE X JAP AIR OUT TO GET
PETER TARES (PT) X WARFIELD KELLY EACH ACKNOWLEDGE
AND ADVISE NUMBER OF BOATS THEY WILL OPERATE TONIGHT
X RICE ACKNOWLEDGE.

To Warfield it was obvious that CTF 31 must have had good
reason to believe that the Japanese were carrying out a large
movement toward Kolombangara that night. For CTF 31 to
throw Arleigh Burke and six destroyers plus all available PTs,
Kelly's at Rice Anchorage as well as Warfield's, into action in
the same general area indicated that something quite serious was
afoot. In point of numbers this would be one of the large PT
actions of World War II.

There was something else about the order too. Never again
was Warfield likely to receive a message that would so soon
spring so violently to life as the line about the Japanese planes
being "out to get Peter Tares." He had had the message in his
hand only a short time when the radioman notified him, "We're
on Condition Red, sir."

Scarcely had the wail of the Rendova siren reached Lumberi
when the tat-tat-tat-tat-tat of machine-gun fire ripped down
through the palm trees. Around the tents bullets flicked up
sprouts of sand. Black puffs of anti-aircraft fire polka-dotted
the sky.

The heavy shoes of cursing men crunched on the coral gravel
in a scramble for cover. Tents were torn by bullets. Here and
there an airplane wing flitted across an opening in the trees. Several officers gathered near the operations dugout stuck out their

necks like scurrying geese and flapped through the brush to foxholes. A rotund, tobacco-chewing employee of the Packard Motor Company, who had been made a warrant officer and sent out to oversee maintenance of the PT engines, dived into a hole that had been dug without any reference to his waistline. With the air vibrant with that uniquely vicious sound of airplane engines and machine guns, the Packard man was horridly exposed to one of war's worst calamities until someone had the mercy to step on him. As he disappeared into the ground, four other officers simultaneously rammed into the narrow entrance to the operations dugout and somehow managed to push inside without pulling it or themselves apart.

Aboard PT 109 the air-raid siren startled Pappy McMahon from a nap on deck by the engine-room hatch. He scrambled to his feet in alarm and saw a plane slanting down on the harbor from the near side of Rendova's mountain wall. "A Marine Grumman!" he murmured with relief.

Even as he said it the plane did a curious thing for a friendly aircraft. It rolled over into a dive, and when it tilted, McMahon saw the Rising Sun on the tail. He turned cold as ice. The plane seemed to be coming straight at PT 109, growing larger every second. At his side he always kept an old Enfield 30-30 rifle that he had picked up somewhere when another man had carelessly laid it down. McMahon depended on that rifle for just the kind of predicament he was in now. But his hand could not find it. Frantically, he groped about the deck, searching with his fingers but never with his eyes. As dearly as he wanted that rifle he could not take his gaze off a black bomb he saw underneath the wing of the plane.

"If I don't keep watching it," he thought illogically, "I'll be hit."

Zinser was struck by the danger when he heard someone shout, "Condition Red." A cry of "Dive bombers!" followed, and the quiet was shattered by the monstrous hammering of the machine guns firing from the decks of all the PT boats. Zinser rushed to help with the cartridge belts.

An enemy plane, diving through the fire from the boats, burst into flame and crashed off Lumberi with a force that raised a sheet of water and held it almost motionless against the trees. Lt. Berndtson on the shore looked down into the clear water and saw the wreckage and the mangled body of the pilot, still presiding with unquestioned authority over the controls.

The sight that most horrified Radioman Maguire was a geyser of water and smoke that bounced out of the harbor in the distance near PT 103, whose own radioman was Bill Maguire, his younger brother.

"*We*'re okay," John Maguire shouted, hoping to hear, "So are we." But PT 103 was nearly half a mile away, and no one heard. Or at least no one answered.

At practically the same moment that he heard the siren Harris saw a group of five or six dive bombers sweeping down from the direction of Rendova Peak. Appalled that the enemy was almost overhead before he knew it, he ran to his battle station at the 20-millimeter anti-aircraft gun on the stern. The gun was not loaded, but with the help of Andrew Jackson Kirksey, Harris inserted a drum of ammunition and opened fire not at the nearest plane but at another that his eyes had been following from the beginning.

Marney, who had come aboard only a few days before, leaped into the forward gun turret and pressed both his thumbs against the trigger bar of the twin .50-caliber machine guns. The guns roared, spitting flame from their barrels and jabbing hundreds of jolts back into Marney's fists and arms.

A bomber streaked close to the water and fired a torpedo into the midst of the boats. Nosing dangerously close to some of them, the torpedo for some reason curved out toward Blanche Channel. Then it circled around and slid up on the beach near a searchlight battery on Lumberi, adding to the fear of the men ashore. Its propeller kept spinning, but fortunately the torpedo did not explode.

Kennedy, who had been waiting for the carpenters when the planes attacked, scrambled into the cockpit and ordered the engines started. "Cast off," he shouted to Maguire.

Smoke and spray spread across the harbor. Overhead there was a terrific flash of flame. A dive bomber plunged straight downward, crashing into one of the PT nests. PT 164, the same one that had survived the strafing by B-25s, blew up, and its load of spare parts flew into the water. Two of the crew were killed. PT 117 was left sinking, and the third was damaged slightly.

Still the planes came. Official reports were to place the number as high as twenty-five, though the sailors did not see that many at one time. One of Marney's guns jammed, but he kept firing the other. Mauer, standing on deck behind the turret, saw the tracers curving away from their target, and he surmised that the jammed gun was dragging the one that was firing.

"Clear that gun!" he yelled to Marney. "Clear that gun!"

"Get down, Mauer," Ensign Thom shouted to him. "Do you want to get killed?"

Mauer threw himself on the deck beside the forward port torpedo tube. He could see the splash of bullets in the water near the boat. A plane passed so low that the face of the Japanese pilot was visible to him.

Shoving his throttles forward to get clear of the concentration of boats, Kennedy steered through a harbor in chaos. In a heavy rumble of engines the undamaged boats were dispersing. The nest that was hit by the plane was in shambles. Gear floated on the surface. Men were swimming. One of them, otherwise apparently unharmed, was covered with gray paint.

While PT 109 zigzagged down the harbor away from Lumberi, the din overhead began to subside, as the planes retired toward the northwest. When the all-clear sounded, Kennedy returned to the buoy, where he and his men took stock of the toll exacted by the bombers. For Maguire at least there was consolation. He could see that his brother and the rest of the crew of PT 103 were safe.

Kennedy rowed ashore in a skiff for the daily conference of boat captains in the operations dugout. On this afternoon it was a solemn affair. Commander Warfield in khaki pants and a khaki shirt open at the neck stood in front of some maps with Lt. Berndtson at his side and asked for a tally of casualties and damage.

"It looks as if the Japs mean business this time," he said. "This is going to be a real big night."

To the skippers who were seated around him on chairs and on the ground he read parts of the CTF 31 message: INDICATIONS EXPRESS MAY RUN TONIGHT . . . Then he read, WARFIELD OPERATE MAXIMUM NUMBER PETER TARES.

"We've got to use everything we have," he said. "How many boats are in condition?"

The skippers whose boats had escaped serious damage reported. Fifteen were in satisfactory shape. Four had primitive radar sets, and Warfield proceeded to form a division around each of these boats.

Each of the four divisions was given a particular area to cover. Division "C" under Lt. George E. Cookman in PT 107 would patrol south of Ferguson Passage to intercept any ships that might attempt to use that channel into Blackett Strait. The other three divisions were to move through Ferguson Passage and patrol in the strait.

Division "R" under Lt. Russell W. Rome in PT 174 was to patrol east of Makuti Island, while the other two would patrol off the south shore of Kolombangara.

Thus Division "A" under Lt. Berndtson in PT 171 would patrol opposite the village of Gatere, and Division "B" under Lt. Henry J. Brantingham in PT 159 would patrol off the village of Vanga Vanga. The station of Division "B," therefore, would be the farthest up in Blackett Strait. In addition to Lt. Brantingham it included, in order, Lt. (jg) William F. Liebenow, Jr.'s PT 157; Lt. (jg) John R. Lowrey's PT 162, and Lt. Kennedy's PT 109. "Oak Zero" was the radio code of the PT base. Each boat was assigned a radio call number. Kennedy's was "Oak 14."

Being the senior skipper, Brantingham was the leader not only of his own division but of the entire group. At twenty-six he had already had a lively career afloat. After graduating from Annapolis in 1939 he sailed in the old four-stacker *Twiggs* until, as one of fifty over-age destroyers, she was turned over to the British at Halifax. After some time in the neutrality patrol in the Atlantic he transferred to PT boats and wound up in Manila in the celebrated Squadron 3. As executive officer of Kelly's PT 35 he was a member of the three-boat expedition that spirited General MacArthur and his wife and son to the north coast of Mindanao in Bulkeley's PT 41. He came to the Solomons in Kelly's Squadron 9.

On the map Warfield indicated how the disposition of the fifteen boats should be adequate to cover every possible approach to Vila through Blackett Strait. If, on the other hand, the Japanese should go around the north side of Kolombangara, then it would be up to Captain Burke and Commander Kelly to intercept them.

"Those of you who weren't supposed to be going out tonight will have to get ready in a hurry," Warfield said. "Better get to it."

Walking back to the skiff, Kennedy encountered his acquaintance from the Melville touch-football field, Ensign George Henry Robertson Ross, a strapping, amiable, artless, popular man, whom his Class of '41 at Princeton had voted "Best-natured," "Most entertaining" and "Worst dressed."

"How about letting me ride with you tonight, Jack?" Ross asked. Formerly executive officer of 166, the PT that had been sunk by the B-25s on July 20 with an alternate crew aboard, Ross had no boat at the moment.

"Do you know how to fire a 37-millimeter anti-tank gun?"
Kennedy inquired.

"Hell no, but I can learn," Ross said.

"Okay, come along then," Kennedy said.

Ensign Ross was twenty-five and from Highland Park, outside
of Chicago. As a boy Ross was taken on visits to his mother's
birthplace at Largs on the Firth of Clyde, where he became
interested in boats. When he was older he used to race scows on
Lake Geneva in Wisconsin and sail on Lake Michigan.

At Princeton he was in the Triangle Show and was the
intramural heavyweight boxing champion. In that pugilistic
era of Tony Canzoneri, Henry Armstrong and Barney Ross it
was inevitable that intramural boxer George Ross should be
called Barney, a nickname that was to cling to him long after
Princeton.

Henry Robertson, whose name he bore, was his mother's
brother, killed while fighting with the Canadians at Ypres just
before Ross was born. When Barney joined the Navy he
became uneasy about his middle name. "I had a superstition," he
explained later, "that because I was named after a man killed in
battle a Japanese bullet was waiting for me out there." Vaguely,
this superstition was mixed up in his motives for asking to
accompany Kennedy. He felt that he needed all the experience
he could get to see him safely through the war. He also wanted
to get away from the base at this time of frequent air raids. Like
nearly every PT sailor, Ross felt more secure aboard a boat,
despite all the hazards of combat at sea.

Kennedy and Ross tramped through the rotting palm fronds
and coconut husks toward the dock on Lumberi. Kennedy was
carrying his charts, and Ross was talking about the turmoil of
the air raid. They walked past gun emplacements fortified with
chunks of coral, where the gunners were still busy restoring
their weapons from the duel with the Japanese planes. Skippers
on their way back to their boats were gathered on the beach. It

was sultry, and the flies were bad. Kennedy and Ross climbed
into a skiff, and Ross rowed them out to the boat. When they
pulled alongside Kennedy hopped aboard PT 109 and handed his
charts to Mauer.

"We're going out tonight," he said.

"*Tonight!*" someone groaned.

"Let's get ready," Lt. Kennedy ordered. "We'll be shoving off
at 1630."

SINCE NOON the *Amagiri, Hagikaze, Arashi* and *Shigure* had
covered many miles. As the sun was descending in the west
they steamed through Bougainville Strait between Bougainville and Choiseul. The constant threat of American planes had
kept the crews alert throughout the day. Now that dusk was
approaching and they were moving down into the Slot, tension became severe. Crisp orders had dispatched every man to
his battle station.

Aboard the *Amagiri* Commander Hanami remained on the
bridge continuously, giving orders and shifting his gaze back and
forth between the horizon and the three other destroyers he
was there to protect. With him on the bridge was a superior officer, Captain Katsumori Yamashiro, commander of the 11th
Destroyer Flotilla. Of the four destroyers the *Amagiri* was the only
one from the 11th Flotilla, and Captain Yamashiro, an officer of
proven valor and considerable combat experience, had come
along as its representative. Forty-four years of age, he had been
born into a naval family at the base at Yokosuka, had graduated
from Etajima in 1919 and for some years thereafter had commanded a gunboat at Canton. He took part in the conquest of
Hong Kong, transported troops to Guadalcanal, and just a month
before took over the 11th Flotilla. While he was the senior officer aboard the *Amagiri* on the present mission, the normal responsibilities of a skipper rested in the hands of Commander Hanami.

The sailors were wearing their tropical uniforms of short-sleeved khaki shirts, knee-length shorts, and caps. In spite of the tension and the hardships of recent weeks their morale was stable and their health normal. Lt. (jg) Akira Nakajima, the *Amagiri's* medical officer, an even-tempered, bespectacled graduate of the Imperial University† Medical School, was not overtaxed. While the ship had been undergoing repairs after Kula Gulf, the crew was hit by a wave of dysentery that wilted thirty officers and men and was blamed on a bad supply of water, but they were back on their feet by the time the "Express" sailed.

The water supply at Rabaul was inadequate at best. The *Amagiri's* crew was under strict limitations on the consumption of drinking water and under severe restrictions on water for bathing and laundering. The worst complaint, however, was over food. The losses that American submarines were inflicting on Japanese shipping had severely reduced the flow of supplies into New Britain. The base crews often managed to divert the best food that got through to their own messes, and there were no stars in Michelin for what was left over for the destroyers. The *Amagiri* had rice enough, and tea. But the men had almost no fresh meat or vegetables, and bread was unheard of. On the trip to Vila the sailors' chopsticks had a different fare to work on—canned bamboo shoots—but the bamboo shoots had been much too heavily salted.

The ship was clean and discipline was excellent. Most of the officers and men had sailed in the *Amagiri* before and knew well enough what challenges they might encounter before the sun would rise again. There were exceptions, of course. Seaman 1/c Seijiro Morimoto, for example, was not particularly worried on his first trip. He had been indoctrinated with the idea that Americans would fight only for money, and thus he was confident that they would be no match for men who fought for the Emperor.

---

†Now Tokyo University.

At dusk the four destroyers, clear of Bougainville Strait, were steaming down the Slot toward Vella Lavella. Their course would take them near Kundurumbangara Point, due south into Vella Gulf, and through Blackett Strait. If they were to be turned back, it would not be the task of Captain Burke or Commander Kelly.

SEVEN

DUSK FALLS EARLY in the Solomon Islands. By 6:15 the sun had dropped low behind Lumberi Island. Palms became silhouettes of giant pinwheels. The still surface of Rendova Harbor turned from blue to flaming gold to cool gray. For a few moments the cumulus clouds hung golden in the west. Then by 6:20 the glare was gone from the sunset. A breeze came up from the northwest and ruffled the water. Objects on shore grew more distinct in the twilight. In particular the whitish trunks of the palms stood out against the deep green of the foliage. Moist gray clouds crept down the darkening summit of Rendova Peak.

At 6:30 the harbor awoke to the cough and thunder of starting engines. There were fifteen PT boats, each with three engines of twelve cylinders each. Forty-five engines beat the kettledrums of a rumbling symphony. Five hundred and forty cylinders throbbed. On a wooden platform at Todd City a sailor snapped his semaphores, and watched for an answer from a signalman on the deck of one of the PTs.

On PT 109 Marney and Harris had uncovered the guns and were loading them. During the air raid the locking pin on the 20-millimeter anti-aircraft gun had broken. Harris suggested that he go ashore for another one, but Lt. Kennedy told him a piece of rope would do to hold the gun in position while the boat was under way that night. "We can get a new pin tomorrow," he said.

In the engine room McMahon was having his nightly problems with the auxiliary generator and was worrying, as usual, about the fuel supply and the batteries. Maguire was busy "locking" his radio on the right frequency and checking all the electrical circuits.

The Japanese dive bombers had wiped out the plans for permanently fastening the 37-millimeter gun and the planks to the foredeck during the afternoon. Kennedy still hoped to try the gun if a target presented itself during the night, but lest the rock of the boat topple it overboard, he ordered the men to lash it to the deck with a rope. He also had them lash down the planks, a small chore for which they would give large thanks later on.

Kennedy showed Ensign Ross about the boat and told him that his battle station would be on the foredeck, where he would serve as lookout and 37-millimeter gunner. Watching them, some of the crew remembered that a visitor was an ill omen.

After putting away the last of the dinner dishes, Mauer was having a cup of coffee in the charthouse with Kirksey. Kirksey's hands were trembling so that he had to set the cup on the chart table and sip the coffee. Kirksey was regarded by the others as a brave man, as bold and steady as any of them. Within the last few days, however, an unshakable conviction that he was going to be killed had taken possession of him. When someone said that the phonograph was too loud, he asked what difference it made: he would soon be dead anyhow. He had a premonition of death that no one could dispel. The air raid and the casualties that afternoon gave it an utter finality.

"Will you take care of my things?" Kirksey asked Harris.

"You're nuts," Harris replied, kindly.

"I won't be going home," Kirksey said.

"You're *nuts*," Harris laughed.

Maguire urged Kirksey to beg off the patrol that night. There would be no fuss about it, Maguire said. Everyone who had been out as much as they had would understand. It would make no difference in his standing with the crew. Kirksey refused. Maguire asked Kennedy to talk to Kirksey, which he did after coming aboard. He tried to encourage him and reassure him, but to no avail.

"I think you ought to stay ashore tonight," Mauer told Kirksey over the coffee. "No one will make anything of it. You'll be okay in the morning."

"They'd say I'm yellow," Kirksey replied. Along with the others he pulled on his kapok life jacket, strapped on his side arms and placed his helmet where he could reach it in case of general quarters.

"Wind her up," Kennedy ordered.

Zinser, who had the watch below, started the engines. Then, after ordering "Cast off," Kennedy shoved his three throttles forward. "Ahead" registered on the annunciators in the engine room, and Zinser, grasping the large gears, engaged the three engines one by one. Kennedy pulled away from the buoy at idling speed. The skippers moved slowly through the harbor to reduce the effect of bow waves on one another.

The boats were mustering by division, and Kennedy wound through the traffic to fall in behind PT 159, PT 157 and PT 162 in Lt. Brantingham's Division "B."

The noisy milling of the fifteen PTs into formation made a stirring sight of war. The sleek green boats were dangerous-looking. Their torpedo tubes were full, their guns aimed at the sky. Their antennae quivered, their engines growled. Their helmeted crews hunched in their kapoks.

The divisions departed in the order of the distances they had to travel to reach their stations. Consequently, Lt. Brantingham's four boats, having been assigned the station on the Kolombangara coast off Vanga Vanga, moved out first.

Through the crisscrossing wakes and vapors from the spluttering exhausts, the four boats rumbled down the harbor and out past Lumberi. Curving into Blanche Channel, their prows lifted in the sweep of increasing speed. In the charthouse Mauer suddenly discovered that in the afternoon's confusion he had neglected to turn in the daily muster sheet to the base. Headquarters, therefore, had no official written record of the names of the thirteen officers and men aboard PT 109 that night.

The three other divisions followed. They all moved in column open order, a broken formation that kept each boat out of the wake of the boat ahead.

At 6:45 the sky brightened in the final glow of the setting sun, and then the light faded swiftly. The low coastal hills of New Georgia grew indistinct off the starboard beam. Astern the crest of Rendova Peak was enshrouded in a low cloud bank, but in the evening sky above it the Southern Cross appeared like a dim kite.

The stars would not remain visible long. As the boats rolled through the stretch of open sea leading to Ferguson Passage a dark overcast was spreading. By the time they entered Blackett Strait the night was like tar.

IN THE ENTIRE SOUTH PACIFIC no place was darker and lonelier than the knob of jungle on Kolombangara several hundred feet above Blackett Strait where Lt. Arthur Reginald Evans, an Australian coastwatcher, peered from his lair into the black void.

Lt. Evans was a courageous man on a dangerous mission of spying on the enemy. In his hideaway overlooking the Japanese base at Vila he had a split-bamboo hut, stocked with rations. He had binoculars and a telescope. He had a compass and a log book. He had a revolver, a captured Japanese rifle and a tommy gun. Above all, he had a radio.

As a member of the network of coastwatchers stretching throughout the Solomon Islands and New Guinea Lt. Evans immediately reported to Lunga, Guadalcanal, every enemy ship or plane or troop movement that his eyes or ears, or those of his native scouts, could detect. His messages, like those of the coastwatchers on other lonely islands, were relayed at once to CTF 31. Time and again this meant that anchor chains would rattle up in Tulagi Harbor or destroyers would turn about in their course or planes would streak down the runway at Henderson Field.

Dear as it was, the Allied victory in the South Pacific would have been much costlier without the help of a few hundred Australian coastwatchers, whose intelligence web was thinly spun out over more than a half-million square miles of Melanesia.

The American planes that shot to pieces the Japanese bombers dispatched to oppose the invasion of Guadalcanal were on the wing because of a warning radioed by a coastwatcher on Malabita Hill on Bougainville. From a Bougainville coastwatcher came the first warning of the great April 7 air raid, a report that gave Allied ships time to disperse before the planes appeared. Coastwatchers detected the Japanese build-up for the attempted reconquest of Guadalcanal. They effectively kept CTF 31 apprised of enemy ship movements in the Shortland Islands. The night PT 112 was sunk under Lt. Westholm the PT boats were in position to damage the destroyer *Hatsukaze* because of a New Georgia coastwatcher's report that a "Tokyo Express" was highballing down the Slot.

Countless Allied airmen, who parachuted or crashed in the islands, and sailors, including some from the *Helena*, whose ships went down, were rescued by the coastwatchers and their network of native scouts.

The coastwatcher service was started just after World War I as a civilian enterprise, conceived and directed by the Australian Navy. With most of the population of the island continent concentrated in the southeast corner, Australia had vast stretches of coastline where an enemy might land without the government's knowing of it for hours or perhaps days. In 1919, therefore, the Navy hit upon the idea of enlisting people like postmasters, harbor masters, schoolteachers, missionaries, police and railway officials—in short, anyone in a position to pass information by telegraph—in an organization whose purpose was to keep an eye out for suspicious occurrences along the coast. The General Post Office agreed to send their reports over telegraph lines to Melbourne, and coastwatchers were given printed instructions on what to report and how.

An important extension of the service was undertaken when Australian administrative officials in New Guinea and the Solomons were enrolled as coastwatchers. After Pearl Harbor the coastwatcher service became an arm of the Navy, and coastwatchers were spirited behind enemy lines by plane, submarine and native canoe.

Every possible effort was made to conceal this apparatus from the Japanese, who hunted the individual coastwatchers mercilessly, sometimes with dogs. The code name for the organization was "Ferdinand," after Munro Leaf's lovable bull who liked to sit under a tree and smell wild flowers. Like Ferdinand, the coastwatchers were supposed to sit and gather information, not fight. Men like Lt. Evans, however, were officers of the Australian Navy.

Reg Evans was a slight, brisk, lithe man with a fair complexion and a long, narrow face. He was cool of temperament, cultivated, and generously endowed with wit and charm. The son of a civil servant, he was born in Sydney on May 14, 1905, the eldest of three children. After attending state schools he went out to the New Hebrides in 1929 as an assistant manager of a coconut plantation. After a French company bought the plantation, young Evans returned to Australia and got a job with the Burns Philp (South Sea) Company, Limited, traders and shippers. This time he was sent out to the Solomons where he held a variety of positions, including, for a couple of years, that of supercargo on the interisland steamer *Mamutu*.

During these years Evans acquired a good deal of knowledge about the Solomon Islands and the Melanesian natives. He also acquired a wife, Gertrude Slaney of Adelaide, Australia, whom he met while she was vacationing with friends in Tulagi.

When Evans became a coastwatcher, he chose his wife's initials, G.S.E., as his radio call letters, and thus Gertrude Slaney Evans won a footnote in the history of World War II.

At the onset of war Evans joined the Army and served for two years in the Middle East. It was not until July 1942 that he was transferred to the Navy and commissioned in the coastwatcher organization. After a stint on Guadalcanal he received orders in February 1943 to open a station on Kolombangara, to which he moved by stages. A PBY picked him up at Florida Island and put him down in the darkness at Segi Point at the southeastern tip of New Georgia, which was still in enemy hands.

The coastwatcher at Segi Point was a tough, resourceful New Zealander named Donald C. Kennedy. Donald Kennedy not only had a following of natives that had been capable of ambushing more than a hundred Japanese soldiers who had ventured too close to his lair but he also had a seagoing force that sailed in schooners. In his ten-ton "flagship" *Dadavata* he once rammed a Japanese whaleboat and blasted the crew with hand grenades. He and his men were credited with the killing of three bargeloads of enemy soldiers, the capture of twenty Japanese pilots and the rescue of twenty-two American pilots. Donald Kennedy got results from his standing offer to the natives of a bag of rice and some tinned meat for every downed pilot, Allied or Japanese, brought alive to his headquarters.

For two weeks Lt. Evans took charge at Segi Point while Donald Kennedy visited Guadalcanal. Then on his return Evans embarked for Kolombangara in a dugout canoe with a native helper named Malanga, who had picked up some English in a mission school. Traveling by night and hiding by day, they passed so close to the Munda airstrip that they could hear Japanese trucks in the darkness. Lt. D. C. Horton, the coastwatcher on Rendova, had sent scouts to Kolombangara ahead of Evans to notify the natives he was coming. As a result a friendly delegation, including Rovu, the ancient headman, met him and built him the hut on the knob on the south shore.

From this height he could look not only down upon Vila, but out across Blackett Strait and Ferguson Passage to Wana Wana and Gizo. He could, that is, when it was light. On this black night of August 1–2, 1943, he could see nothing but the dial of his watch.

BY 9:30 P.M. the fifteen boats from Rendova were on their respective stations, idling or merely lying to. Division "C" was patrolling outside Ferguson Passage. The others, having cleared the passage, were patrolling in Blackett Strait. This is a large body of water. Blackett Strait and the waterways, particularly Vella Gulf, that flow into it form a basin twenty-four miles long from Wana Wana to Vella Lavella. The basin is a minimum of five miles wide. This narrowest point, where most of the boats were concentrated, lies between Kolombangara and the small islands scattered east of Gizo.

As the hours passed, the boats idled or drifted in pairs through the calm black water. Division "B" moved in two sections. Lt. Brantingham's PT 159 was paired with Lt. Liebenow's PT 157; Lt. Lowrey's PT 162 was paired with Lt. Kennedy's PT 109. Brantingham and Lowrey were the leaders of their respective sections.

Aboard PT 109 Kennedy was still at the wheel with Maguire at his side. Occasionally Ensign Thom would lean over the cockpit and shoot the breeze with the skipper. As on other evenings, Maguire would turn to Kennedy with some such question as, "What was Churchill like?" The conversation would consume a few minutes and then everyone would fall silent again.

The crew was tense, but most of the men had little to do except to watch and wait. While the boats were on radio silence, the scratching of static could be heard on the open receiver. From time to time Maguire would say his rosary. Ensign Ross chatted off and on with Albert, whom he had known at Lumberi. Otherwise he knew no one aboard except Kennedy and Ensign Thom. McMahon, Johnston and Zinser alternated on duty in the engine room. The boat was running well, although after many weeks away from drydock she was not so frisky as she had been at Tulagi. Her hull had, as the sailors said, "a heavy beard," meaning a growth of sea moss that accumulates in tropical waters when there is no opportunity for scraping the bottom.

Men on watch noted the passing of midnight. It was now Monday, August 2.

Lt. Brantingham was standing anxiously by the cockpit of PT 159 when he heard a voice below call, "Radar contact!" Turning around to a ladder into the charthouse, Brantingham dropped below and saw a column of four luminous spots on the radar screen. They were so close to the shore and looked so small that he guessed they were enemy barges. He estimated that they were two or three miles away.

Since the crude radar set was of little use in tracking vessels, Brantingham scurried up to the deck and looked in the direction of the spots. Unable to see a thing in the blackness, he went down for a second look at the screen. Within the space of a few minutes he shot up and down the ladder half a dozen times.

He could tell that the spots were drawing steadily closer. He still believed, however, that they were barges, and he ordered his boat to make a strafing attack.

"Keep your fire low," he instructed the gunners on PT 159. The tendency was to shoot over barges in the darkness.

The confusion that was to strangle the whole PT operation that night was already well under way. The four spots were not barges, but the *Amagiri*, *Hagikaze*, *Arashi* and *Shigure*, the punctual Japanese destroyers only minutes away from their destination at Vila.

When Brantingham launched his attack, moreover, practically all of the other PT boats were left in complete ignorance of the fact. Either the 159 crew did not break radio silence to notify the other skippers or poor communications swallowed the message. In any case Kennedy, having no radar of his own and hearing no message, had no idea that enemy ships were near. Neither did he know that Brantingham had taken off on an attack. Most of the other skippers were equally uninformed.

As Brantingham moved in to strafe, the Japanese opened fire. The heavy caliber of their guns immediately identified the ships as destroyers. Brantingham abruptly abandoned the idea of strafing. At eighteen hundred yards he pressed two chest-high buttons on the cockpit panel. Two torpedoes leaped from their tubes. A moment later he pressed two other buttons. Two more torpedoes lunged into the sea. In those days the PTs carried obsolete Mark VIII torpedoes. Brantingham's not only missed their target, but one of them set the lubricating grease in its tube afire, lighting up PT 159.

Meanwhile his section-mate, Lt. Liebenow in PT 157, caught sight of two of the destroyers and joined Brantingham in the attack. He fired two torpedoes, but they also missed. By now the Japanese had a target in 159's blazing torpedo tube, and it was all Brantingham and Liebenow could do to escape alive, turning and twisting at high speed and laying down puffs of smoke to confuse the enemy gunners. The puffs thrown out by smoke generators on the fantails looked in the distance like boats and made it more difficult for the enemy to ascertain the true target. By the time 159 and 157 were out of range they had raced clear across Blackett into Gizo Strait.

As the destroyers sailed on unharmed past Gatere on the way to Vila they flickered into the radar screen aboard PT 171, the lead boat of Lt. Berndtson's Division "A." Unaware that Division "B" had made an attack, Berndtson sensed that the greenish dots on the screen were the "Express." He ordered the skipper, Ensign William Cullen Battle of Charlottesville, Virginia, to close in at ten knots for a torpedo strike. At fifteen hundred yards Berndtson fired four torpedoes at the second destroyer in line. To his horror all four of the torpedo tubes caught fire. The destroyer seemed to turn toward Berndtson to allow the torpedoes to slide by and then opened fire on him. With shells whistling in so close that the crew was splashed with water, PT 171 tore across Blackett Strait and out to sea through Gizo Strait. The three other boats in Division "A" received no report of any contact with enemy destroyers.

The experiences of Divisions "R" and "C" were much the same. They, too, fired a good many torpedoes, but to no effect. Although a total of thirty torpedoes were fired by the four divisions, the *Amagiri, Hagikaze, Arashi* and *Shigure* pushed on to Vila without a scratch.[†]

While all this was taking place, Kennedy was continuing his uneventful patrol, paired with Lowrey in PT 162. The instructions were that Lowrey was to keep tuned to Brantingham by

---

[†]In his three-volume *A History of Motor Torpedo Boats in the United States Navy*, prepared in the Office of Naval History, Commander Robert J. Bulkley, Jr. (not to be confused with Lt. John D. Bulkeley), observes: "This was perhaps the most confused and least effectively executed action the PTs had been in.... The chief fault of the PTs was that they didn't pass the word. Each attacked independently, leaving the others to discover the enemy for themselves."

TBY radio and that Kennedy was to stay close enough to receive from him any orders that Brantingham might issue. Lowrey, however, did not know any more than Kennedy did that Brantingham and Liebenow had charged off on an attack.

They and their crews knew that something was happening because in toward Kolombangara they could see flashes and star shells. Not realizing that enemy destroyers were passing, they guessed that Japanese shore batteries might be firing on the PT boats. When the beam of a searchlight from one of the destroyers swept close to 109 and a couple of shells burst nearby, the men feared that the coastal guns were getting range of them. Kennedy called "general quarters," and the crew went to battle stations.

Under the circumstances Lowrey swung away from Kolombangara and slipped up Blackett Strait toward Vella Lavella. Following his section leader, Kennedy pulled close enough to ask Lowrey if he had any word on what was going on. Lowrey replied that he had not. Shore batteries were probably firing, he said. Nevertheless on 109's radio the men could hear occasional exchanges like, "I am being chased through Ferguson Passage. Have fired fish." "Well, get the hell out of there." Obviously, some of the boats were engaged at sea somewhere.

As Lowrey and Kennedy were easing their way up Blackett Strait, Lt. Potter's PT 169 from Division "A" emerged out of the darkness and joined them. Since Berndtson had been driven off by the destroyers on the heels of Brantingham, Potter had lost contact with the remaining two boats of his division, just as Lowrey and Kennedy had lost contact with their division, now broken up by the retirement of Brantingham and Liebenow.

With the tactical plans thus utterly scrambled, Kennedy, Lowrey and Potter lay to out in the strait to await developments. It was so dark that they had a difficult time remaining in contact with one another. Finally, they decided to call Rendova, thirty-eight miles away, for instructions. An order came back on the radio to resume patrol. Lowrey was uncertain of the direction from which they had come, and at his request Kennedy led the way back to where he believed they had started, namely, in the vicinity of Vanga Vanga.

This new group began patrolling to and fro on station, each boat rumbling along on one engine. As a result of their briefing the skippers knew that Japanese ships were expected, but not a man aboard any of the three boats knew that four enemy destroyers had passed through and would soon be returning on their way back to Rabaul.

EIGHT

When the "Express" reached Vila around 12:30 A.M. the *Hagikaze, Arashi* and *Shigure* lay to in lower Blackett Strait a thousand yards from shore to unload. The *Amagiri*, which in Japanese means "Heavenly Mist," dropped off behind them to guard against any attack through the narrow neck of the strait between Kolombangara and Arundel Island.

From Kolombangara dozens of barges and landing craft swarmed out around the three drifting destroyers like junks around freighters in Hong Kong harbor. Sailors heaved cases of food and ammunition overboard onto their decks. Soldiers swung down landing nets.

The whole operation took place under the most intense pressure for haste. With their engines dead the destroyers would be easy targets for enemy ships, planes or submarines. Also, the sailors, looking ahead, wanted to get away as quickly as possible so as to be out of range of American fighter planes when daylight came.

"Hurry, hurry!" they kept exhorting the debarking troops. The soldiers, stumbling about on dark stairs and decks, resented the abrupt treatment they were getting. Why should they be in a vast hurry? *They* weren't going back to Rabaul.

In spite of the grumbling and confusion the unloading was

carried off with dispatch in darkness broken only here and there by downward-pointed masked flashlights in the hands of petty officers. On each of the three destroyers four parties of twenty-five sailors went to work on the stores of cargo. These crews were stationed fore and aft on each side of the ships. Barges lined up at these stations. The sailors would toss along boxes and crates until a barge was full. Then the loaded barge would pull out and another would move up in its place.

On the bridges of the destroyers were hooded signal lamps, with each ship's lamp masked in a different, identifying color. Less than an hour after their arrival the dim red lamp on the *Hagikaze* signaled: "Let's go home." Nine hundred soldiers and more than seventy tons of supplies were already ashore or on their way to the shore in barges.

The destroyers' engines were started. After allowing five minutes for warming them up, Captain Kaju Sugiure in the flagship *Hagikaze* gave the signal to get under way. Although there was every reason to suppose that PT boats would still be lurking up in Blackett Strait, the Japanese nevertheless preferred this route around the southern shore of Kolombangara to the risk of going out through Kula Gulf and meeting destroyers or cruisers. They did not know that Captain Burke was waiting north of Kolombangara, with six destroyers, but experience suggested as much. To whatever extent Japanese sailors were harassed by PT boats, they preferred to deal with them than with the heavy guns of cruisers and destroyers.

The forty-five minutes or so that the other destroyers had spent at Vila were anxious ones for Commander Hanami on the covered bridge of the *Amagiri*. Cruising back and forth across lower Blackett Strait, he was constantly worried that a PT boat, a destroyer or even a PBY would discover him.

While the islands around him were held by his own troops, these narrow waters were treacherous for Japanese ships. Anywhere he turned Commander Hanami knew that an American man-of-war might be waiting. Navigating in the dark was dangerous because of the reefs. There were no adequate charts for this area of the Solomons. Furthermore, the *Amagiri* carried no radar. To a degree this disadvantage was offset by a group of trained lookouts who searched the darkness through ten affixed, wide-angle night binoculars.

It was with great relief that Commander Hanami finally received a signal from Captain Sugiure that the *Hagikaze, Arashi* and *Shigure* were starting back up the Kolombangara coast. He immediately ordered the coxswain to head northwestward at increasing speed to rejoin them.

Approximately in his path several miles distant was PT 109, with Kennedy steering away from Kolombangara in a westerly direction toward Gizo, following PT 162 and PT 169. Kennedy had no orders other than to patrol off Vanga Vanga and to look for whatever he could find. His mission boiled down to a matter of guessing where in the impenetrable blackness he might find a target.

Encountering no sign of enemy ships in the middle of Blackett Strait, Kennedy made a fateful decision. He overtook Potter and Lowrey and suggested that the three boats reverse their direction. He believed they would have a better chance of rejoining the missing boats if they returned to the vicinity in which they had all been scattered in the first place. The other two skippers agreed. The three boats turned about and with Kennedy now in the lead headed toward the southeast, the direction from which the Heavenly Mist was blowing at a speed of thirty knots.

Commander Hanami strained forward from the starboard side of the *Amagiri*'s bridge, impatient for the broader passage of Vella Gulf. Captain Yamashiro paced the port side. Between them stood Lt. (jg) Hiroshi Hosaka, the torpedo officer, constantly checking the readiness of his own crews. The wheel was in the hands of Coxswain Kazuto Doi.

The ship was still on general quarters. Lookouts hunched against the binoculars. Lt. Nakajima, the medical officer, waited in his quarters behind the bridge. Petty Officer 2/c Mitsuaki Sawada gazed out an open window in the forward gun turret, wondering whether they would make it back to Rabaul without trouble. Lt. (jg) Shigeo Kanazawa, a gunnery officer, was poised on the cover of the bridge.

Aboard PT 109 Ensign Ross was standing on the foredeck by the 37-millimeter gun. Behind him was Kennedy at the wheel. At the skipper's right was Maguire and just beyond and above Maguire was Marney in the forward gun turret. On the skipper's left, outside the cockpit, was Ensign Thom, lying on the deck. Standing behind the cockpit was Mauer. Aware that Kennedy still hoped to meet some of the other dispersed PT boats that must be wandering about the strait, Mauer was peering through the night for a familiar form.

Albert was on watch amidships. Harris, off duty, was sleeping on the deck between the day-room canopy and a starboard torpedo tube. He had removed his kapok jacket and was using it as a pillow. McMahon was on watch in the engine room. Johnston was dozing on the starboard side of the deck near the engine-room hatch. Zinser was standing close by. Starkey was the lookout in the after gun turret. Kirksey, off duty, was lying aft on the starboard side.

The boat was moving so quietly that Ross, scanning the dark, could barely hear the idling engine above the soft sound of the breeze and the splash of water against the bow. He had the sensation of gliding in a sailboat, and he was gratified that they were in deep enough water that he would not have to worry about reefs for a while.

"Ship ahead!" a lookout shouted to Commander Hanami.

"Look again," Hanami ordered.

"Ship at two o'clock!" Marney shouted to Kennedy from the gun turret.

Kennedy glanced obliquely off his starboard bow. Ross was already pointing to a shape suddenly sculptured out of the darkness behind a phosphorescent bow wave. For a few unregainable moments Kennedy thought it was one of the scattered PT boats. So did Mauer. So also did some of the crews of PT 162 and PT 169, who sighted the *Amagiri* at about the same time or perhaps seconds earlier. As the shape grew, Kennedy and Mauer quickly recognized that it was not a PT boat. On PT 169 Potter called a warning on the radio, but it either was not received aboard 109 or else arrived too late.

"Lenny," Kennedy said in a matter-of-fact voice, "look at this."

Ensign Thom stood up,

What followed took place within the span of perhaps forty seconds or less.

In the *Amagiri's* forward gun turret Petty Officer Sawada received an order: "Fire!" The destroyer was already so close to the smaller boat, however, that he could not depress the guns in time to aim.

On the foredeck of PT 109 Ross frantically grabbed a shell and rammed it at the 37-millimeter. It slammed against a closed breech. He knew he would never have time to load.

Commander Hanami, now recognizing the American vessel as a PT boat, decided that his best protection would be to ram.

"Hard a-starboard," he called.†

Coxswain Doi, informed that the object ahead was a PT, expected just such an order on the strength of what he had

---

†Years later Captain Yamashiro said that *he* ordered "Hard a-port" and that subsequent events were accidental. This has caused a profound controversy in Japan since Mr. Kennedy's election and, needless to say, the most delicate relationship between Hanami and Yamashiro. On the basis of the detailed statements made to me by the crews of PT 109 and the *Amagiri* the case for an accidental ramming is difficult to sustain. Coxswain Doi said, "Captain Yamashiro does not remain much in my memory."

heard discussed about the best tactics in such a situation. He turned the wheel about 10 degrees to starboard.

To Ross the destroyer originally appeared to be traveling on a parallel course. Now he distinctly saw the slender mast heel toward PT 109, indicating that the destroyer was turning in his direction.

"Sound general quarters," Kennedy told Maguire.

Maguire turned around, took a couple of steps out of the cockpit and yelled, "General quarters!"

"We're on general quarters," Albert said to Starkey. Starkey's battle station was the after starboard torpedo, so he climbed down from the port gun turret and started across the deck.

Back in the cockpit, Maguire fingered a Miraculous Medal suspended from a chain around his neck. Ross crouched under the bow gun.

On the bridge of the *Amagiri* Lt. Hosaka considered ordering his torpedo crews to fire, then decided it would be useless. PT 109 was too close. Torpedoes would pass under her.

Kennedy spun his wheel in an instinctive attempt to make a torpedo attack on the *Amagiri*. The torpedoes, however, would not have exploded even if they had struck the destroyer, because they were not set to fire at such a short distance. Moreover, PT 109, idling on a single engine, was moving so sluggishly that there was no chance to maneuver against the swiftness of the destroyer.

Seeing what was coming, Maguire grasped his Miraculous Medal and had begun to say, "Mary, conceived without sin, pray for us . . ." when the steel prow of the *Amagiri* crashed at a sharp angle into the starboard side of PT 109 beside the cockpit.

Harold Marney, the newcomer, the youth who was taking the wounded Kowal's place in the forward turret, was crushed to death, probably at the moment of impact, and his body never found.

The wheel was torn out of Kennedy's grasp as he was hurled

against the rear wall of the cockpit, his once-sprained back slamming against a steel reinforcing brace. It was the angle of the collision alone that saved him from being crushed to death with Marney. The destroyer, smashing through the gun turret, sliced diagonally behind the cockpit only several feet from the prostrate skipper. Helplessly looking up, Kennedy could see the monstrous hull sweeping past him through his boat, splintering her and cleaving the forepart away from the starboard side of the stern.

In the engine room McMahon had had no warning of danger. He was standing among the engines, casually touching the manifolds to make sure they were not getting too hot and regulating the scoop controls, which fed sea water through the cooling system. From time to time, as a means of getting optimum functioning, he would alternate the engine on which the boat was running.

Something on one of the gauges caught his attention, and he was climbing over machinery to look at it when a tremendous jolt flung him sideways against the starboard bulkhead and toppled him into a sitting position alongside an auxiliary generator. In disbelief he saw a river of red fire cascading into the engine room from the day room. His reason told him that this was impossible because a hatch separated the two rooms, and he himself had dogged it down before leaving Rendova. It did not occur to him that the hatch and most of the bulkhead had been sheared away and the gasoline tanks over the day room had been ignited by friction sparks or a broken electrical cable.

The river of fire rose about him. It seared his hands and face and scorched his shins, exposed by his rolled-up dungarees. He held his breath to keep the flames from his lungs. He was fairly engulfed in a world of blinding light and roasting heat and then without any transition he was immersed in a watery darkness, his lungs almost bursting. Sheared away by the destroyer, the flaming stern was pulled down by the weight of the engines.

Without the sensation of descent, McMahon found himself under water fighting to get to the surface, which appeared from below as a wavering orange glare. Bobbing to the top at last in his kapok, he emerged in a sea of fire. The burning gasoline was spreading across the water in a garish patch of light that could be seen by Lt. Evans on his hilltop a few miles away. He knew that a ship must be on fire, and he supposed he might hear more about it in time.

Johnston's plight was scarcely less desperate than McMahon's. In his sleep he was knocked into the sea in his heavy Army shoes, steel helmet, blue shirt, socks, dungarees and kapok. He opened his eyes to see the sliding hull of the destroyer. Looking up in shock he saw Japanese sailors running on the deck. As the *Amagiri*'s stern swept by him the suction of the screws yanked him under the surface. The downward churn of the water spun him head over heels into the depth like a piece of clothing in a washing machine.

Johnston wondered if he was doomed. He did not pray, but he thought of his wife, Nathalie. As the descending currents released him, he pulled his way upward. The struggle seemed hopeless. He did not know how far under he was. He decided to give up and die. Then he thought that his wife would consider him a coward, and he resumed his toil. The pain in his lungs was excruciating. Seeing no light, he feared he was still near the bottom. Giving up would be easy now, even desirable. Again, however, the thought crossed his mind, "Nat will think I'm yellow." He resumed the climb on his watery ladder. Faintly the orange glow flickered above his straining face. Now determined to survive, he thrashed his way to the top, gasping for breath and beating the flames away with his hands.

As the *Amagiri* ripped through PT 109 Captain Yamashiro smelled something that reminded him of smoldering cotton. Lt. Hosaka could feel heat on the bridge. Petty Officer Yoshitaka Yamazaki, a medical corpsman, had been crossing the deck to the sick bay when he heard someone shout that a PT boat lay ahead. He felt a thud, saw a burst of flame and was stabbed with the thought that the Americans had fired a torpedo into the *Amagiri*.

"What's happened?" Petty Officer Masayoshi Takashima called from his torpedo station.

"The port side's afire," Shigeo Takemura shouted up to the bridge. Takemura, a communications man with a torpedo crew, thought that the enemy's torpedomen had succeeded in doing what the *Amagiri*'s had failed to try. He supposed the flames were pouring out of the destroyer.

In the starboard engine room Petty Officer Shigeo Yoshikawa felt a shock. Lt. Shigeru Nishinosome noticed that the ship's engines were starting to shake. In the port engine room Petty Officer Yoshiji Hiramatsu heard a scraping noise against the hull and feared the *Amagiri* had hit a reef. He observed that the starboard propeller shaft was vibrating. In the auxiliary engine room Petty Officer Takao Tan heard a thud and hastened up to the deck, thinking they had been hit by a torpedo.

As the *Amagiri* swept on she fired two shots back at PT 109, but both missed. By now the vibration was so severe that Hanami had to reduce his speed to investigate the trouble. Part of a blade of the starboard propeller had been sheared off, causing the shaft to shake. Also, the bow was dented. This was the extent of the damage, however, and no one was hurt.

Hanami found that by lowering his speed to twenty-eight knots he could sail without excessive vibration. In answer to an inquiry from the *Hagikaze* about the fire he radioed to the other three ships that he had sunk a PT boat. Wild cheers swept through the *Shigure*. Their mission a complete success, the four destroyers returned to Rabaul.[†]

[†]Eight months later, shortly after Commander Hanami was transferred from the ship, the *Amagiri* was sunk with considerable loss of life by a magnetic mine in the Makassar Strait off Balikpapan, Borneo.

THOUGH HURLED ABOUT by the crash, Kennedy, Ross, Mauer and Maguire were still on the bow, which was kept afloat by its watertight compartments. Mauer was thrown to the deck, bruising his right shoulder. Maguire was flung out of the cockpit back against the day-room canopy. His helmet was pushed down on his brow, but he pried it off in time to see the *Amagiri* passing through behind him.

As the impact of the destroyer tilted the deck sharply to port, Ross let go of the loose bow gun for fear it would topple overboard and carry him to the bottom. He mistook the first flare of flames for a bright searchlight. Thinking the enemy was about to fire down on them, he slipped off the starboard side into the water and hid in the shade of the hull. Gasoline fumes choked him, and he fainted.

Pulling himself up from the corner of the cockpit, Kennedy's first thought was that a gasoline tank might explode from the heat. "Everybody into the water," he yelled.

"Wait for me," Maguire pleaded. His rubber lifebelt had failed to inflate. An extra kapok was in the charthouse, but he was afraid of being left alone aboard. Kennedy waited until he had fetched it, then, putting his hand on some debris, vaulted overboard. Maguire and Mauer went in with him. Kennedy did not feel any pain, and at the point where he entered the water the flames had been washed aside by the *Amagiri*'s wake.

As the three swam out a safe distance, the forepart of PT 109 was left a battered, deserted hulk, drifting in two hundred fathoms through the glare and hiss of flames. The stern had already disappeared.

Andrew Jackson Kirksey, the quiet Georgian with the strong premonition of death, had perished with Marney. Kirksey had been lying on the starboard side from which the destroyer came and toward the stern. He might have been killed on impact and hurled yards into the water or he might have been crushed and gone down with the stern. No one knew. Ensign Thom,

McMahon, Johnston, Albert, Harris, Starkey and Zinser were, like Ensign Ross, floating about in fire or fumes, some of them unconscious.

Harris, his head pillowed on his kapok on deck, had been awakened by a shout to worse than a nightmare. He saw what looked to be an enormous prow knifing straight at him only feet away. He sprang up and dived sideways over the torpedo tube, and while he was still in the air the *Amagiri* crunched into PT 109. Some part of the boat, perhaps the tube, snapped up and struck him in the left thigh, painfully knocking him several yards beyond where a dive would have carried him. Somersaulting through the dark, he could see fire break out. Then he landed in the water in a sitting position, astonished and thankful to find that he had his kapok on, untied.

A moment before it had been his pillow. Now it was wrapped around his chest, keeping him afloat. In the instant between jumping up and diving he must have pulled it on, but he had no recollection of doing so. Shaking the salt water out of his eyes he saw the stern of the destroyer vanishing into the dark and heard two shots.

Neither Zinser nor Starkey ever saw the *Amagiri*. On deck Zinser heard the cry of "General quarters" and the next thing he knew he was flying through space. For a moment he could see flames. Then he fainted. While walking toward his battle station at the after starboard torpedo tube, Starkey was sent reeling. He thought they had been hit by a shell. His helmet knocked off, he toppled into one of the smashed quarters, which was lighted up by flames. He thought that this was what hell must be like, and then he lapsed into unconsciousness.

As the fire on the water around the boat subsided, Kennedy concluded that there would be no explosion. He and Maguire and Mauer swam back to the bow of the boat and climbed up on the deck. At Kennedy's direction Mauer got out the blinker, a two-foot-long tube with a light inside, and started walking around the hulk, flashing the light periodically as a beacon to any members of the crew who might still be alive in the water.

Apart from Maguire and Mauer, Kennedy did not know what had become of his crew. He was impatient for the other boats to come to his aid, but they never appeared. Just before the collision PT 162 had attempted an attack on the *Amagiri*, but Lowrey's torpedoes did not fire, and he turned away to the southwest. Just after the collision, PT 169 fired two torpedoes to no effect, whereupon Potter moved out of the vicinity. Presumably skippers of other boats thought that the crew of PT 109 had perished in the flames and that Blackett Strait was no place for loitering with Japanese destroyers steaming through.† As the hours—and years for that matter—passed, the men on PT 109 were bitter that they were not rescued, yet their bitterness never focused on any one man or any one boat.

As soon as Mauer was ready with the blinker, Kennedy removed his shoes, shirt and sidearms and dived overboard in a rubber lifebelt to search for the others. He was to be in the water approximately thirty of the next thirty-six hours. Fortunately, it was warm and calm.

On the hulk Maguire and Mauer received the first inkling that others were alive when they heard Zinser's voice in the darkness calling, "Mr. Thom is drowning. Bring the boat!" Dreading to swim back into the fumes, Maguire nevertheless got a line from the rope locker on the bow. He tied one end to a broken torpedo tube and the other end around his waist. With a prayer he stepped into the water and swam toward the sound of Zinser's voice, leaving Mauer, shipwrecked for the second

---

†In his magazine article "Survival" John Hersey says that one of the skippers, whom he does not identify, put his hands over his face and sobbed, "My God! My God!" The official record shows only two PT boats patrolling with 109 that night: PT 162, whose skipper, Lt. Lowrey, is dead, and PT 169, whose skipper, Lt. Potter, says he has no recollection of making any such outcry.

time in three months, a solitary figure afloat on what was left of PT 109.

Ross, having fainted in the bright light of the flames, awoke in darkness, wondering where he was and what he was doing. As his head cleared, he saw two men not far from him. Swimming over to them, he found that one was Zinser, whom he did not know by name, and the other was Thom. Zinser was moaning. Thom was gibbering. When Ross shook him, Thom reached out his huge arm and tried to climb up on him as if he were a log. Fending him off, Ross cried, "Lenny, Lenny, it's me!" After some sparring in the water Thom came to and appeared to be in good condition. Zinser was all right too, and they started to shout for the others.

Maguire was swimming toward them. The gasoline fumes nearly suffocated him, and he prayed that he would not faint. He had no difficulty finding the men because of their voices.

"Are you all right, Mr. Thom?" he asked.

"I'm all right," Thom said.

"Can you keep going?"

"I can make it."

Maguire could see that Zinser did not need any help beyond an occasional tug he was getting from Ross. Guided by the blinking of Mauer's light, Maguire, Ross, Zinser and Thom swam slowly back to the boat, where Albert presently splashed out of the night to join them.

After leaping into the water just in time to escape being crushed by the *Amagiri*, Harris drifted off alone. At first he felt severe pain in his left leg from the blow he had received while diving, but in time his leg grew numb and he could not use it. Bobbing about in his kapok, Harris supposed that he was the sole survivor. This thought haunted him until he saw someone drifting out of the flames sixty feet away. With his own left leg dragging, Harris swam laboriously toward the man, whom he could not recognize because he was floating with his helmet partially covering his face. The man evidently was in such a state of shock that Harris could not even recognize his voice, although he could make out that the man was saying that he could not use his hands and was appealing for help to get his helmet off. It was only when Harris pried the helmet loose that he recognized Pat McMahon. The night was too dark for Harris to see well, but he could tell that McMahon was in serious condition.

Not knowing what to do or where to go, Harris treaded water by McMahon's side. Once the fire had burned out, the night was blacker than ever. Harris believed that he and McMahon were the only two alive, and he could not imagine what would become of them. The thought that the others were dead had taken such a hold on him that he was startled when he heard voices somewhere.

"Mr. Kennedy!" he yelled. "Mr. Kennedy!"

"Over here," he heard Kennedy call back.

"McMahon is badly hurt," Harris told him.

"I'm over here," Kennedy shouted. "Where are you?"

"This way," Harris called. He could hear the splashing of Kennedy's arms and legs. It sounded far off. Periodically, Kennedy would pause and call, "Where are you?" and Harris would answer "Over here." Harris heard the splashing grow louder, and then he saw Kennedy's head coming out of the dark. McMahon lay helpless in his kapok. Despite the cooling effect of the water his whole body felt warm.

"McMahon is too hurt to swim," Harris told Kennedy.

"All right, I'll take him back," Kennedy said. "Part of the boat is still floating."

Kennedy did not mention any other names, but the sound of voices in the distance lifted Harris's spirits. McMahon, however, was without hope. He could not use his arms at all.

"Go on, skipper," the crew's "old man" mumbled to Kennedy. "You go on. I've had it."

Kennedy clutched McMahon's kapok and began towing him toward the boat, which by this time had drifted a considerable distance from the swimmers. The men aboard kept calling to give their position, and Kennedy followed the sound. At first Harris stayed abreast of Kennedy and McMahon despite his numb leg. Then, his strength on the wane, he dropped behind. "Come on," Kennedy urged him. Harris resumed swimming, but the burden seemed unendurable. His left leg dragged. He was drowsy. It felt luxurious just to slump back in his kapok and drift. Drawing farther and farther away, Kennedy would call back to him, and he would respond by lifting his heavy arms to swim awhile. Then, tiring, he would drift again. It had been cool on deck and before taking a nap he had pulled a sweater on above his jacket and his shirt. The weight of his clothes and his shoes anchored him. "The hell with it," he would say to himself. He no longer could hear Kennedy, but this did not seem to make any difference to him any more. When he had the strength he would swim; when he did not, he would go limp and say "The hell with it."

It seemed as though he was alone for a half-hour or longer before he again heard Kennedy splashing toward him, calling, "Where are you, Harris?" As Kennedy reappeared, Harris wearily told him, "I can't go any further."

"For a guy from Boston, you're certainly putting up a great exhibition out here, Harris," Kennedy snapped.

Harris cursed and swore at Kennedy. He was aggrieved that Kennedy did not realize how much his leg troubled him. "Well, come on," Kennedy persisted. Harris asked the skipper to hold him up while he took off his kapok to shed his sweater and jacket. Kennedy gripped his arm and held him precariously on the surface. Had the exhausted and dispirited Harris slipped from Kennedy's grasp he might have gone down like a stone. But with his heavy clothes and his shoes off and his kapok back on, Harris found he could move through the water, and he and Kennedy swam slowly back to the boat.

Thom, meanwhile, was having even greater difficulty rescuing Johnston. When Johnston had come gasping to the surface after escaping from the churning propellers, he swallowed gasoline and inhaled fumes. Retching forced more fumes into his lungs. His brain became clouded. He was confused, violently sick and semiconscious. His neck was burned. He saw the floating bow and men on it. When he called out, Thom heard him and swam to his side. By this time, however, Johnston was almost helpless. At Thom's urging he would kick a few times or try the dog-paddle, but it was so much easier to sleep.

"Come on, Bill, let's go," Thom would say, shaking him. Johnston would kick for a while and then fall back to sleep, not caring whether he ever reached the boat.

"Let's keep paddling," Thom pleaded. He himself was only a fair swimmer, and it took him a long time to drag Johnston to the floating bow.

Starkey was among the last to make it. The part of the boat into which he had been flung by the crash quickly filled with water and he floated free. The thought that he was all alone surrounded by Japanese frightened him. So did the danger of sharks. "Oh my God. Oh my God," he kept saying. He floated without being able to make up his mind what he should do until he saw some debris near him. He climbed up on a mattress. His face and hands were burned, though not severely. As he lay on the mattress, he thought of his wife, Camille, and four-year-old daughter, Shirley, and he remembered the day he had enlisted after Pearl Harbor. Then he saw the dark outlines of the boat. It looked a couple of hundred yards away at least, but the sight gave him courage. He took off his shoes and swam to rejoin the others, who were either lying on deck or drifting in the water, hanging on to the hull.

Kennedy called the names of the crew. Everyone answered but Marney and Kirksey. He inquired whether anyone had seen them or had any idea what had happened to them. No one had. Kennedy called, "Kirksey . . . Marney . . ." From time to time during the night others kept repeating the call, but there was never any answer.

All the survivors seemed to be in fair condition except McMahon and Johnston. Both of McMahon's hands were covered with third-degree burns, and his face, arms, legs and feet were burned. In the water the burns had glowed warmly, but when the men lifted him up on deck he felt as if his whole body were on fire. He took off some of his clothes to relieve the friction on his burned skin. Despite the terrible surface heat, however, he became so cold that he had to put the wet clothing back on.

Johnston was alternately unconscious and wracked by spells of vomiting. He did not speak, and the others were at a loss to know what was the matter with him. Maguire thought Johnston was dying. It was a problem to keep him from rolling down the slanting deck into the water. Someone suggested lashing him to the boat, which provoked a long discussion in the dark, because others felt that there would be no way to prevent Johnston from being carried to the bottom if the boat should suddenly sink. In the end some of the men held lines around him for a time, but did not tie them down.

During the long hours of darkness most of the men had climbed up on the hulk and reclined with their feet braced against some fixture to keep them from sliding off the deck. They spoke in low voices about the prospects of rescue after daylight. Some thought PTs would return for them; others guessed that a PBY would pick them up.

When dawn broke over Wana Wana they could see Rendova Peak thirty-eight miles to the south. They knew almost exactly where they were. They knew that the other boats would be back at the base now, that Lumberi would be stirring with the morning's activity and that their absence would set in motion a search that should lead speedily to their rescue. There was already some cause for this optimism.

SWEEPING BLACKETT STRAIT with his binoculars in the early light, coastwatcher Evans saw an object floating near where he had observed the blaze during the night. In his morning report to New Georgia and Guadalcanal, which had the call letters KEN (after Lt. Commander Hugh McKenzie, one of the great coast-watchers, who, from his headquarters in Guadalcanal, commanded the organization's activities in the Solomons), Evans noted:

> . . . ALL FOUR [DESTROYERS] WENT WEST OWE TWO TWO OWE
> X PLANE DROPPED BOMBS NEAR SAMBIA AND LATER NEAR
> GATERE X SMALL VESSEL POSSIBLY BARGE AFIRE OFF GATERE
> AND STILL VISIBLE

At 9:30 A.M., upon receiving notification from the PT base, the coastwatcher near Munda (call letters PWD) informed Evans:

> PT BOAT ONE OWE NINE LOST IN ACTION IN BLACKETT STRAIT
> TWO MILES SW MERESU COVE X CREW OF TWELVE X† RE-
> QUEST ANY INFORMATION

Aboard PT 109 in the meanwhile daylight had substituted the dread of exposure for the terror of darkness. While inflating hopes for rescue, the sunrise had also torn away the protection of night. Rendova Peak was a comforting sight, but it rose far beyond the confines of Blackett Strait. The eleven Americans were encircled by Japanese. They could see buildings on Kolom-

---

†Ross's presence was not taken into account, evidently.

bangara, and Gizo. In particular they looked toward Gizo with apprehension because the briefings at Lumberi had stressed the danger of enemy forces there. The men felt uncomfortably conspicuous on the water. They were only a few miles at most from enemy garrisons on high ground at Kolombangara and Gizo. The Japanese could have seen the hulk as easily as Evans, but unlike Evans they had the means to investigate it or blow it up. So far as Kennedy and the men knew the enemy might already be preparing to come out after them.

"What do you want to do, fight or surrender?" Kennedy asked his crew.

"Fight with what?" someone asked.

They took stock of their weapons. The 37-millimeter gun, still lashed to the deck, had fallen overboard and was hanging uselessly in the water. To Ross it looked like a giant fish lure. Maguire fetched a Thompson sub-machine gun from the charthouse. Among them the men had six .45s and Kennedy still had the .38 that had been issued to him aboard the *Rochambeau*. In addition to the guns there was one large knife, one light knife, and one pocket knife left. The boat's first-aid kit had been lost in the collision.

To lessen their chances of being seen Kennedy slid into the water along the port side and ordered everyone in after him except Johnston and McMahon. He again brought up the question of what should be done if the Japanese came out.

"There's nothing in the book about a situation like this," he said. "A lot of you men have families and some of you have children. What do you want to do? I have nothing to lose."

This struck Maguire as incongruous. He felt that because of his wealth and advantages Kennedy had the most to lose.

McMahon, tormented but clear of mind, was emphatically opposed to surrender. No one favored surrender, because of the tales they now recalled about Japanese torture of prisoners, but some of them questioned whether it would be possible to put up a fight. No one knew for sure whether their sidearms would fire after so many hours in the water. There was no way to dry them.

Mauer said, "If they do come out, we will see them long before they get here. If it seems that we have any chance at all, let's fight. But if they send out three or four barges with enough men to overwhelm us, let's surrender. We're no good to anybody dead." He added, however, that he would do whatever Kennedy ordered.

Zinser also suggested that they make no definite decision until they saw the size of any Japanese force that might come after them. No one had any better suggestion, and this was the way the matter was left. By 10 A.M. the list to starboard had become so acute that the bow turned turtle but remained afloat. The men helped McMahon and Johnston onto the upturned bottom.

At 11:15 A.M. Evans messaged PWD, Munda:

REF YOUR 0930/2 NO SURVIVORS SO FAR X OBJECT STILL
FLOATING BETWEEN MERESU AND GIZO X THREE TORPEDOES
AT VANGA VANGA

When the bow turned turtle Kennedy knew that something would have to be done if they were not rescued soon. The hulk seemed to be settling in the water. If it should sink that night with them still hanging on, they would become separated in the dark, and some would surely drown. On the other hand, if the bow stayed afloat and drifted with the men clinging to it, they would be at the mercy of the currents. For all Kennedy knew they would drift right into the arms of the Japanese. It became increasingly evident that if help did not come within a few hours, he would have to order the men to abandon the boat and swim to shore before dark. The question of what shore to swim to, however, had him in a quandary. What island large enough to conceal eleven men would be free of Japanese troops, even a Japanese observation post?

Now and then he and his men sighted a plane in the distance. In hope that it was an Allied aircraft they would wave, but the plane would drone on, and Kennedy would order them to stop waving lest they attract the enemy.

The men cursed war, they cursed the Navy, they cursed Lumberi, they cursed the PT boats that should have been thundering to their rescue and the planes that should have been circling reassuringly overhead.

"If I ever get out of this," someone vowed, "I'll never ride on a PT boat again."

"A PBY will come soon," Starkey said hopefully.

Harris's left leg was swollen above the knee. Thom examined it, and assured him no bone was broken. The problem of sharks was mentioned casually. Several times since daybreak the men had seen porpoises. Since sharks are thought to stay clear of the leaping, playful porpoises, the sight eased the sailors' minds for the time being.

At 1:12 P.M. Evans received a message from KEN, Guadalcanal:

DEFINITE REPORT PT DESTROYED LAST NIGHT BLACKETT STS
APPROX BETWEEN VANGA VANGA AND GROUP OF ISLANDS SE
OF GIZO X WAS SEEN BURNING AT ONE AM THE CREW NUM-
BERS TWELVE POSSIBILITY OF SOME SURVIVORS LANDING
EITHER VANGA VANGA OR ISLANDS

Someone had it figured out very well indeed.

Kennedy was concentrating on the islands around him. So familiar was he with Blackett Strait that he had no difficulty recognizing them even from water level. About two miles to the east was Kolombangara. Not only was it the base of a considerable number of Japanese forces but it lay at the opposite side of

Blackett Strait from Ferguson Passage and thus was removed from the normal course of the PT boats. The chances of rescue there would be slight.

To the west, about three and a half miles away, was the group of small islands that hang in the shape of an anchor from the southeastern tip of Gizo. The anchor is four or five miles long, and therefore the islands on the arms were well out from under the eyes of the Japanese garrison on Gizo, supposing that no outposts had been established in the small islands. Moreover the reef along the base of the anchor borders Ferguson Passage and would offer a vantage point for trying to signal the PT boats from Rendova at night.

As is typical of the Solomons, almost all of the islands in the anchor are known by more than one name. Each had been called one thing by the European settlers and another by the natives, who speak the Roviana language. Thus one of the principal islands in the shaft of the anchor is called Bambanga, or Long, Island. Below it is Olasana Island. Further below, at the base of the anchor, is Naru,[†] or Cross,[††] Island. The arm of the anchor curving into Blackett Strait is formed by Naru, by a small adjacent sandspit called Leorava, by an insignificant circle known as Three Palm Islet which resembles an island in a shipwreck cartoon and, at the tip, by Plum Pudding, or Kasolo, Island. All are connected by a reef in which there are only one or two openings.

Sometime after one o'clock Kennedy said that they would have to abandon PT 109 and try to get up on land somewhere before dark. He told them that they would head for the island group east of Gizo. There was considerable discussion about which of these islands it would be best to go to. No one relished the risk of swimming ashore, but they agreed that the worst haz-

---

[†]Sometimes spelled *Nauru*.
[††]Sometimes spelled *Gross*.

ard would be staying with the boat too long. Every hour increased the danger of detection.

From the position to which they had drifted since the collision Naru was nearer than any of the other islands, except Leorava and Three Palm Islet, which were too small to conceal eleven men. On the other hand, Naru appeared large enough to Kennedy to have a Japanese outpost, particularly since it looked out directly on Ferguson Passage. He pointed to Plum Pudding Island, so named because of its shape, and said that even though it was somewhat farther away, it was smaller and less likely to contain Japanese than Naru. No matter which he chose it would be a gamble. He decided that they would strike out for Plum Pudding.

Since some of the men were better swimmers than others, Kennedy knew it would be difficult to keep the group together on the long swim. Furthermore McMahon, whose burns were dreadful to look at, was helpless. In getting ready to shove off Kennedy noticed that one of the two-by-eight planks they had placed under the 37-millimeter in Rendova Harbor the day before was still floating by the bow at the end of its rope. This plank, he thought, might solve the problem of separation.

"I'll take McMahon with me," he said. "The rest of you can swim together on this plank. Thom will be in charge."

The men who still had shoes removed them and tied them around the plank. They took the boat's battle lantern, a ten-pound, square gray flashlight, wrapped it in a kapok to keep it afloat and tied the kapok to the plank also. Maguire threw the secret radio code book overboard.

"Will we ever get out of this?" someone asked.

"It can be done," Kennedy told him. "We'll do it."

With a last look at PT 109 they cut the two-by-eight loose from the bow and, buoyed by their kapoks, grouped themselves about the plank, four on one side and four on the other, with a ninth man, often Thom, going back and forth from one end to the other, pushing and pulling at the plank. The men on the sides each threw an arm over the plank and paddled with the other. All of them kicked. Zinser reflected that the kicking would not only hasten their crossing but would tend to scare sharks away. Harris and Maguire still felt they must have been observed. They wondered when the Japanese would come after them. There was no way of putting up a fight now.

McMahon, sure that death was only a matter of time, remained silent when Kennedy helped him into the water, which stung his burns cruelly. In the back of his kapok a three-foot-long strap ran from the top to a buckle near the bottom. Kennedy swam around behind him and tried to unbuckle it, but the strap had grown so stiff from immersion that it wouldn't slide through. McMahon was surprised at the matter-of-fact way Kennedy went about it all. It was as if he did this sort of thing every day. After tugging the strap a few times Kennedy took out his knife and cut it. Then he clamped the loose end in his teeth and began swimming the breast stroke. He and McMahon were back to back. Kennedy was low in the water under McMahon, who was floating along on his back with his head behind Kennedy's.

From Kolombangara at 4:45 P.M. Evans messaged KEN:

THIS COAST BEING SEARCHED X IF ANY LANDED OTHER SIDE
WILL BE PICKED UP BY GIZO SCOUTS X OBJECT NOW DRIFTING
TOWARDS NUSATUPI IS

Evans told his native scouts to pass the word among the islands to be on the lookout for PT boat survivors.

NINE

PLUM PUDDING ISLAND is an oval of green with a band of white sand around it like a life preserver, holding it afloat in water that blends from sapphire, where it is deep, to the color of mint where it washes the coral reefs. The island is about a hundred yards long and seventy yards wide at the middle. A few palms rattle in the breeze, but the place is dominated by tall casuarina trees with long needles. The branches form an unbroken canopy over the sandy ground, carpeted with dead needles. Mats of decaying leaves from the naqi naqi trees give off a sweet odor. Coral fragments lie scattered under the white-flowering kidoki-doga bushes. On the beach are nautilus shells and kauri shells, which because of their cartographic markings are called by the natives, in their own tongue, map-of-the-village shells. Hermit crabs scurry about like tiny Atlases with the world in the form of their shells on their shoulders. Birds, however, are the chief inhabitants. White wading birds waddle along the shore. Frigate birds wheel overhead, and in the evening thousands of black gulls fly back from their searches of the sea to nest in the trees.

Near sundown on August 2 Kennedy and Pat McMahon half drifted up on the southeastern rim of Plum Pudding Island. Reaching the clean white sand seemed to be the ultimate limit of Kennedy's endurance. His aching jaws released the strap of

McMahon's kapok, the end of which was pocked with Kennedy's tooth marks. For a time Kennedy lay panting, his feet in the water and his face on the sand. He would have been completely at the mercy of a single enemy soldier, but the island was deserted. His feet blistered, McMahon crawled out of the water on his knees and feebly helped Kennedy up. Swimming with the strap in his teeth Kennedy had swallowed quantities of salt water. When he stood he vomited until he fell again in exhaustion. McMahon's hands were swollen grotesquely. Every move he made tortured him. He knew, however, that as long as they were on the beach they would be exposed to view. He tried to drag Kennedy across the ten feet of sand, yet he could scarcely drag himself. He found he could crawl, and as Kennedy's strength returned he too crawled across the beach in stages with McMahon until the two of them collapsed under the bushes. After a while Kennedy was strong enough to sit up and watch the others as they neared the beach on their two-by-eight plank.

It took the eleven survivors fully four hours to swim the three and a half miles across Blackett Strait from the overturned hulk of PT 109 to Plum Pudding Island. At the start they were all close together, but gradually Kennedy pulled ahead with McMahon in tow. Kennedy had swum the backstroke on the Harvard swimming team and was generally a strong swimmer. Towing McMahon he would move in spurts, swimming the breast stroke vigorously for ten or fifteen minutes and then pausing to rest.

"How far do we have to go now?" McMahon would inquire. Kennedy would assure him that they were making good progress.

"How do you feel, Mac?" he would ask, and McMahon would invariably reply, "I'm okay, Mr. Kennedy, how about you?"

Being a sensitive person, McMahon would have found the swim unbearable if he had realized that Kennedy was hauling him through three miles or so of water with a bad back. He was miserable enough without knowing it. Floating on his back with his burned hands trailing at his sides, McMahon could see little but the sky and the flattened cone of Kolombangara. He could not see the other men, though while all of them were still together, he could hear them puffing and splashing. He could not see Kennedy but he could feel the tugs forward with each stretch of Kennedy's shoulder muscles and could hear his labored breathing.

McMahon tried kicking now and then but he was extremely weary. The swim seemed endless, and he doubted that it would lead to salvation. He was hungry and thirsty and fearful that they would be attacked by sharks. The awareness that he could do nothing to save himself from the currents, the sharks or the enemy oppressed him. His fate, he well knew, was at the end of a strap in Kennedy's teeth. At that stage of his life it never occurred to him to pray. His sole reliance was on Kennedy's strength.

Thom, Ross, Harris, Johnston, Starkey, Zinser, Albert, Mauer and Maguire found it slow going on the plank. At the outset Ross, a strong swimmer, moved around the log helping the men. "Let's see how you kick," he said to Harris. In spite of his sore leg Harris kicked hard. "You're doing all right," Ross assured him. The plank had little to do with buoying them up. Their kapoks did that. As Kennedy had foreseen, the plank kept them together, and this had a good psychological effect. Occasionally, to be sure, some of the better swimmers became irritated over the pace.

"If we go on like this we'll all be lost," one complained.

"As far as I'm concerned," said Mauer, a poor swimmer, "I'm going to stay here. You swim by yourself if you want to."

"Listen," Thom thundered. "I'm giving orders here. We all stick together."

Then he reconsidered. Perhaps it would be faster without

the plank. He allowed the men to try swimming on their own, but the result was disappointing.

"This isn't getting us anywhere either," Thom said. "Back on the board!"

Instead of tying his shoes to the plank, Ross had hung them around his neck. As the hours passed their weight bothered him, and he dropped them, a thoughtless move he was to regret. Other things were lost, too. Maguire was carrying the submachine gun. After it had been in the water for some time the stock fell off and the remaining metal parts of the weapon were very heavy. Eventually Maguire felt that it was futile to try to hold onto the gun without the stock, and he let it go to the bottom.

The men made no effort to paddle in unison. They just pulled and kicked and wrestled the plank along. It was arduous work, particularly for those who, like Zinser, suffered from burns. Zinser noticed that the blue tattooed girl on his left arm had become a blonde under a blister. For the first time since the collision, however, the men now had a goal, and this brought a sense of relief to some of them. Also they felt less conspicuous away from the boat. No one spoke much. Few had the energy.

Their worries increased as they neared the island. They couldn't be sure they were not swimming into a Japanese trap. As yet they did not know how Kennedy and McMahon had fared. With only a couple of hours of daylight left their hopes of rescue before another night were fading.

As they approached the island finally, Kennedy waved to them from under the trees. When they saw him they felt the relief of men who had come safely through the first round of danger. There was enough of a current flowing by the island to cause them some difficulty in bringing the plank in to the beach. The nastiest part was getting through the coral. Coral antlers jabbed their shins. Coral spurs cut their feet. Coral knobs bruised their thighs. At times the men slipped and cut themselves against beautiful abrasives. At other times the surge of water swept them involuntarily against a coral spike. When they finally dragged the plank up on the beach they looked every inch the part of nine shipwrecked sailors.

The men ducked under the trees near Kennedy and McMahon. There was little conversation. Pulling off their kapoks they all sat breathing heavily and staring across Blackett Strait at Kolombangara.

From his knob five or six miles directly across from them Lt. Evans was getting off his last message of the day. Having seen a flight of Allied planes and assuming they were looking for the survivors, he asked KEN:

WILL YOU PLEASE ADVISE RESULT OF SEARCH BY P FORTYS OVER GIZO

He received no answer that night.

WHO HEARD IT FIRST no one could recall afterward, but suddenly the men were frozen by the sound of a boat approaching from the direction of Ferguson Passage. They threw themselves on their stomachs and crawled up to the bushes bordering the sand. A motorized Japanese barge with three or four men in it was chugging up Blackett Strait only a couple of hundred yards away. Had they seen the swimmers, and were they coming after them? Was this a regular patrol? Would the Japanese head in for a routine reconnaissance of the island? More acutely than ever the American sailors were confronted with the question of what they should do if challenged by superior fire power. Their sub-machine gun was gone now, and the few remaining sidearms were in dubious condition.

The barge moved slowly, but it did not turn. Tensely, the men watched it push past their bushes and head straight for the enemy garrison at Gizo Anchorage some four miles away. If the Japanese had come by only a few minutes earlier they would have caught Kennedy and his men helpless in the water. They could have shot or seized them, as they pleased,

Although the barge passed, the sight of it frightened the men deeply. They were made more keenly aware than ever of their encirclement. How many more barges would pass? Where else might the Japanese be? For all the men knew there were some on the same island with them, and they did not dare to venture more than a short distance from the clump of bushes and the beach. They spoke only in hushed tones.

Harris, the gunner's mate, collected the sidearms, laid them on a damp shirt and took them apart and dried them as best he could. Everyone was obsessed with thoughts of food (they had none) and of rescue. This was all the men talked about as the sun went down. It never occurred to them that they had been all but given up for lost by their comrades. Paul Fay, the ensign Kennedy had threatened with dismissal from the PT service at Melville, who was now at Lumberi, sat down in despair and wrote to his sister: "George Ross has lost his life for a cause that he believed in stronger than any one of us, because he was an idealist in the purest sense. Jack Kennedy, the Ambassador's son, was on the same boat and also lost his life. The man who said that the cream of a nation is lost in war can never be accused of making an overstatement of a very cruel fact."

The three officers, Kennedy, Thom, and Ross, drew aside and conferred among themselves. The question was simply put by Kennedy. "How are we going to get out of here?" As they hashed over the problem, their theory of rescue boiled down almost exclusively to the idea of intercepting the PT boats in Ferguson Passage, difficult though it would be for a swimmer to attract their attention in the dark. Quietly Kennedy said that he would swim out into the passage that night and see what he could do with his revolver and the battle lantern. Ross thought this was absurd. Nevertheless Kennedy broke up the conference and told the other men his plans. To McMahon they seemed suicidal. Maguire urged Kennedy not to go. Kennedy ordered that a watch be kept on the beach during the night.

"If I find a boat," he said, "I'll flash the lantern twice. The password will be 'Roger'; the answer will be 'Willco.'"

He stripped down to his skivvies and strapped the rubber life belt around his waist. He wore shoes to protect his feet on the reefs. He hung the .38 from a lanyard around his neck. The revolver swung at his waist, the muzzle pointing down. He wrapped the battle lantern in a kapok to float it.

Dusk had settled over Blackett Strait when he stepped into the water. He knew that the PT boats would be leaving Rendova Harbor at just about this time. What he did not know was that Warfield had dispatched the boats to the southern tip of Vella Lavella. They would be operating that night not in Ferguson Passage but in Gizo Strait miles to the north.

Through the trees the men watched Kennedy make his way from the shore to the reef. His departure depressed them and made them feel lonelier than ever. Under the direction of Ensign Thom a watch was set up on the beach. Two men would be on at a time, each for two hours. They would crouch on the beach with one man looking in one direction and the other looking the opposite way. Before long Kennedy was a speck disappearing in the water.

The line of the reef bends southward from Plum Pudding along the arm of the anchor, past Three Palm Islet to Leorava, the sandbar next to Naru. Thence, curving around into the outer arm of the anchor, it forms the upper boundary of Ferguson Passage. Kennedy's objective was to follow the reef until, near Leorava, it touches Ferguson Passage and then to leave it and swim out into the passage. The depth of the water along the way varies. Sometimes Kennedy could walk in water

waist-deep or shoulder-deep. At other times the reef would fall
away and he would have to swim until his foot touched it again.
Now and then he would lie on the water and grasp coral out-
croppings and pull himself along to spare his legs,

As darkness came on it was an eery trek. Often when he put
his foot down something darted away in the water. He could tell
that the reef was alive with creatures strange to him. Once he
saw a huge fish and winced at the recollection of tales he had
heard of the mutilation of men by sharks and barracuda. He
flashed his light and thrashed his arms and legs. The fish swam
away. The coral bottom was slippery. Occasionally Kennedy
would slip against a fascicle of coral and cut his leg. At other
times he would step unwittingly into a deep hole and go under.

After nightfall Blackett Strait was lonelier than a desert. As
landmarks disappeared, Kennedy's sense of direction blurred.
Phosphorescent particles blinked at him from the water. The
only sounds were the whistle of the breeze and the lapping of
the waves. Though the water was warm, Kennedy would often
feel cold. The blotting out of points of reference by the darkness made it difficult for him to know how fast he was moving, how far he had gone, how far he had yet to go. His only
map was the reef. When he would reach a break in it he would
have to swim through deep water, hoping that in the blackness
he could pick it up again on the other side of the gap.

Stumbling, slipping, swimming along, he finally reached Ferguson Passage after having traveled a distance of between two
and three miles. Pausing to rest, he took off his shoes and tied
them to his life belt. Then he floated off the reef and struck out
for the center of Ferguson Passage, towing the battle lantern
along in the kapok. With the .38 trailing below him in the water,
the lanyard tugged at his neck as he swam.

Out in the Ferguson Passage he treaded water, looking
toward the Solomon Sea and listening. It was his intention,
when the PTs came through, to fire a recognition signal of three

shots into the air, and flash his light at the nearest boat. The skipper would be the most surprised sailor in the South Pacific to find Jack Kennedy paddling around by himself in the middle of the Passage. This comforting dream never came true. Instead of PT boats, Kennedy saw only aerial flares beyond Gizo. Did this mean, he wondered, that the boats had gone up west of Gizo and were operating in Gizo Strait? As hours passed and none appeared he concluded that this must be the case.

Foggy and tired from his long hours in the water, he faced back toward the reefs and started swimming again. His limbs were lifeless. To lighten his burden he untied his shoes from the lifebelt and let them sink, though he knew what a slashing his feet would take when he got back on the reef. As he swam he wondered, however, whether he was ever going to get back. He moved on and on through the darkness but he never seemed to come to the reef. What was happening apparently was that a current through Ferguson Passage was carrying him sideways into Blackett Strait.

On the beach at Plum Pudding sometime after midnight, Harris, while standing watch, thought he saw a light on the water and was electrified by hope that Kennedy had attracted a PT boat and was coming to their rescue. In all probability Kennedy was miles away and the light was phosphorescence or the reflection of a star. It was not necessarily a product of Harris's imagination alone, however, because when he roused the other men some of them saw it too—or thought they did. Thom strode out into the water, calling, "Jack! Jack!" Some thought a voice answered. As the minutes passed the men began to ask themselves whether what they had seen and heard was real, or whether they had seen and heard what they had wanted. In any case time went by and Kennedy did not come. Faintly in the distance they could hear the pounding of the ocean on the reef beyond Naru. A shower drenched the island and the thirsty men licked the leaves. The rainwater tasted bitter. The

leaves were coated with bird droppings. In days to come the survivors would give Plum Pudding, or Kasolo, Island a third
name—Bird Island.

The discovery Kennedy made with his weary wits when daylight came was that in spite of a debilitating expenditure of
energy he was still wallowing about at the confluence of Ferguson Passage and Blackett Strait. As dawn spread a pale light
on the water, he was able to reorient himself. He had just
enough strength left to make it back to Leorava. Crawling up on
the sands of the tiny island with one tree and a patch of bushes,
he collapsed in a deep slumber.

DURING THE LONG DARK HOURS that Kennedy had been swimming through the wastes of Ferguson Passage the Japanese had
landed from two to three hundred more soldiers at Kequlavata
Bay on the northern coast of Gizo Island. Some of the Gizo
Scouts—the natives who were working for Lt. Evans—had a
camp at Sepo Island, between Plum Pudding and the site of the
landing, and they spotted the Japanese reinforcements. They
knew that they must carry this intelligence to the coastwatcher.
Early on the morning of Tuesday, August 3, therefore, Biuku
Gasa and Eroni Kumana climbed into a dugout canoe and paddled down Blackett Strait on a mission as simple as any in the
greatest of all wars could possibly be. Yet by a most extraordinary
combination of circumstances this mission was destined to result
in the saving of eleven officers and men of the United States
Navy, one of whom would become the President of the United
States within the lifetime of Biuku and Eroni.

Biuku and Eroni were ebony-colored Melanesians of slight
stature but superb form. Eroni's face wore a stern, intense
expression, while Biuku looked blithe and gentle. Both youths
were around nineteen. Biuku had been born on Wana Wana
Island and briefly had attended a Methodist mission school run

by the Australians. Religion affected him. Although he understood little English, he could say, "In God we trust" with more
meaning than the phrase carries on most lips. Eroni was born
in Lale Village on Ganongga Island and also had received instructions before the war in a Methodist school. Like Biuku, he
was loyal to the British and was willing to help Britain's allies
when war burst into the Solomon Islands.

The two young natives paddled for a long time without seeing anything unusual except some flotsam off Bambanga Island.
They fished out of the water a box that contained a razor, a
shaving brush, a tube of shaving cream and a handwritten letter, which they could not read. They carried the letter with
them. In a brief pause at Wana Wana they showed it to Benjamin
Kevu, an older scout, who read and spoke English well, having
been an employee of the British post office at Gizo before the
Japanese invasion. Benjamin observed that the letter was signed
by Raymond Albert. He had no idea who Albert was or where
he had come from, and the letter meant nothing to him. From
Wana Wana, Biuku and Eroni moved on by canoe to report to
Lt. Evans on Kolombangara.

Tuesday, August 3, was to be a busy day for Evans. After an
overnight wait for his inquiry about the findings of the P-40s
over Gizo, he was first informed that the planes had not been on
a search but were merely passing by on an unrelated mission.
Later PWD, New Georgia, corrected this in a message to Evans,
referring to him by his call letters:

AIRINTEL HERE HAVE REQUESTED US TO TELL GSE A SEARCH
WAS MADE YESTERDAY DUSK WITH NEGATIVE RESULT

The failure of the planes to locate survivors compounded the
problem. If an air search could not locate the missing men, what
justification did Warfield have at this stage of the campaign for
risking boats in enemy waters looking for them? Ensign Battle

had wanted to go back up into Blackett Strait during the day on August 2 in PT 171. He might well have found the eleven survivors while they were still clinging to the hulk of PT 109. Under the circumstances, however, he was denied permission. If Evans could see the floating bow, which, presumably, is what he saw, how could planes fail to spot eleven men on a clear day in a body of water only about five and a half miles wide at that point? The explanation evidently lies in the report of Air Intelligence that the search was made at dusk. In other words, in the endless confusion surrounding this event, the search was delayed so long that by the time the planes reached the Gizo area the survivors were hidden under the trees on Plum Pudding Island.

Evans had no better word for his base than his base had for him. He messaged KEN:

SEARCH NEGATIVE EXCEPT ONE MORE TORPEDO AT PILPILI

As Biuku and Eroni were on their way to Kolombangara Kennedy woke up in broad daylight on Leorava. He felt cold and utterly ragged and still had a mile and three-quarters to swim to return to his men. He tried the battle lantern but it did not light, so he tossed it aside. His shoes having been discarded the night before, he waded back into the water in his skivvies with only his lifebelt and revolver. The coral cut his bare feet as he started back up the reef.

When Kennedy had failed to return at daybreak, the men grew discouraged. They feared he had drowned. Johnston was still in a haze, and McMahon's pain was awful. Periodically he soaked his burns in salt water. It stung like fire, but he felt he had to try something. Mauer, nagged by hunger and thirst, decided to try climbing a tall palm to get some coconuts. Part way up a large red ant bit his leg and he had to slide down and pull the ant off like a chigger. On the next attempt he made it to the top and twisted off three unripe coconuts, one of which, upon returning to the ground, he pried open with great effort with his knife. Parched from his exertions, he drank the bland, warm water. Johnston asked if he could give McMahon a drink.

"Yeah, there are two of them," Mauer replied, pointing to the other coconuts on the ground.

When Mauer had finished drinking, Thom gave him a cutting look and asked sarcastically, "Have you had enough?" At that Mauer glanced down at the uncomplaining McMahon, and realizing that neither Johnston nor McMahon had the strength to open a coconut, he was covered with remorse. He could not understand what had happened to him, that he had not offered them a drink.

Harris had been concerned over the lack of oil for the pistols, and the coconuts gave him an idea. He knew there was oil in coconut meat, so he disassembled all the .45s and rubbed it on the moving parts. The experiment was not successful because the coconut meat had a gummy effect on steel.

As the men were lying in the bushes late in the morning idly watching the gulls fish in Blackett Strait, Maguire suddenly exclaimed, "Here's Kirksey!" When he looked again he saw that it was not Kirksey but Kennedy swimming in from the reef. Thom ordered the men to stay under cover while he and Ross went to meet him. Ross threw his arms around Kennedy, but Kennedy fell to the beach, retching. He looked skinny, bedraggled and exhausted. He had a beard. His hair was matted over his forehead. His circled eyes were bloodshot. His sun tan had taken on a yellowish hue. Thom and Ross dragged him across the sand into the bushes. When Maguire asked him how he felt, he grunted. After a while someone inquired whether he had seen any PT boats. "No," he said. He muttered something about being unable to control his movement in the currents. He became very sick and then fell asleep. The others could think

of nothing to do. They sat there as the afternoon wore on. Once
Kennedy woke, looked up at Ross and said, "Barney, you try it
tonight," and then went back to sleep.

Ross was convinced of the futility of swimming into Ferguson Passage, but he obeyed. Warned by Kennedy's ordeal, he
set out at four o'clock in order to reach the passage while it
was still daylight. The channel was just a marking on charts to
him, and he wanted to get his bearings so he could surely find
his way back. That was his chief worry. He was afraid he would
get lost among the islands. He told the others not to expect
him that night unless he succeeded in signaling a boat. If his
mission should prove unfruitful, he would remain on one of
the reef islands until daylight. He took Kennedy's Smith & Wesson on the lanyard. Also, to reduce the risk of attracting sharks by
the white shade of his legs he donned khaki pants. As he slithered and swam along the reef, he was appalled to see some sand
sharks three or four feet long. When he reached Ferguson Passage dusk was falling. Since it was still too early to go out, he
swam about until his foot touched a coral head where he could
stand in chest-deep water outside the reef. Depressed by the
silence, he occupied himself by making mental notes of the
seascape to guide him back.

Soon it was not only lonely and silent but pitch-dark. Waves
washed him off his pedestal, but he would grope his way back to
wait until he guessed it was time for the PTs to approach. He
dreaded the thought of swimming by himself into Ferguson Passage. He might not have done so had Kennedy not done it the
night before. "If he can do it I can do it," kept running through
Ross's mind.

He swam for about twenty minutes. He was not sure whether
he had gone far enough, but he feared going too far. He treaded
water and waited. He did not know, of course, though he began
to suspect it, that the PT boats had again gone up to Vella Lavella.
He hauled the .38 out of the water and pulled the trigger.

The revolver fired, but the shot sounded flat against the broad surface of the water. At intervals he fired twice more. After a long wait he swam back to the reefs and was happy to discover that he had come in near an islet, which was Leorava, Kennedy's resting place the night before. He went ashore and promptly fell asleep.

On the morning of Wednesday, August 4, he awoke in the warm sun feeling fine. Boyishly, he felt like an emperor of his own realm. He wished the other men could see him and relished the thought of how he would tell people back home about his South Pacific adventures after the war. It was just like a magazine cartoon of a man shipwrecked with a blonde. Except there was no blonde, he reflected. Standing on the sand barefoot in rumpled pants, his hair unkempt and a black beard sprouting from ear to ear, he magnificently confirmed the judgment of the Princeton Class of '41 when it had voted him "Worst dressed."

By the time Ross started swimming back to Plum Pudding, Biuku and Eroni had reached Evans's hilltop with the news of the Japanese landing at Kequlavata Bay. Evans asked them if they had seen or heard of any PT boat survivors in the islands around Gizo. They said they had not, whereupon the coastwatcher at 10:25 A.M. messaged PWD:

NO SURVIVORS FOUND AT GIZO

As they left to return to Sepo Island, the native scouts were reminded by Evans that there might be PT survivors in the Gizo area. At 11:30 A.M. Evans received a message from KEN:

WHERE WAS HULK OF BURNING PT BOAT LAST SEEN X IF STILL FLOATING REQUEST COMPLETE DESTRUCTION X ALSO REQUEST INFORMATION IF ANY JAPS WERE ON OR NEAR FLOATING HULK

Because of other traffic Evans did not reply until 5:05 P.M.
when he messaged KEN:

CANNOT CONFIRM OBJECT SEEN WAS FLOATING HULK OF PT
X OBJECT LAST SEEN APPROX TWO MILES NE BAMBANGA
DRIFTING SOUTH X NOT SEEN SINCE PM SECOND X P FORTYS
FLEW LOW OVER IT AND GIZO SCOUTS HAVE NO KNOWLEDGE
OBJECT OR ANY JAPS THAT VICINITY

Ross had no trouble finding Plum Pudding. When he arrived
during the morning he discovered that Kennedy was feeling
better, although the second consecutive failure to make contact
with the PT boats had a dispiriting effect on everyone. Johnston, showing signs of recovery, was now frightened but tried
not to show it. Starkey was deeply discouraged. He was assailed
by doubts as to whether he had done the right thing by his
family when he enlisted. His brain seethed with questions about
the merits of the Navy, the aims of the United States in the war
and his own purposes in life.

With some quietly, with others openly, bitterness toward the
Navy was growing. "Where are the boats, anyway?" the men
asked. To the other officers, Thom and Ross, Kennedy betrayed
his anger at Lumberi for not making a greater effort at rescuing
them. To the men he did not show it. He never made light of
their predicament, but now and then he would get off some
remark about it that would force a laugh. "What I would give
for a can of grapefruit juice!" he said to Zinser. Now that he had
overcome his exhaustion he kept purposely active. Without
exhorting, he tried to give the men the feeling that he was opti-
mistic, that things would turn out well.

Because of his burned arms Zinser would sometimes feel
sorry for himself—until he looked at McMahon. McMahon's
pitiable condition made everyone ashamed to complain. It broke
Kennedy's heart to look at him. Scabs forming over his burned

eyelids made it difficult for him to see. The palms of his hands were swollen to a thickness of three inches. They were cracked like burned bacon, and he could look deeply into his own flesh. His misery was redoubled because his burns were giving off a terrible stench, which he knew was offensive to the others. He did not seek the help of God, but in his pain he reflected that if he ever got home, he would do things differently. Still, he was less sure than ever that he would see his home again.

The men were hungry. Mauer had last fed them late on Sunday afternoon, and it was now midday Wednesday. Partly because he wanted more coconuts for the crew to eat and partly because he wished to be nearer Ferguson Passage and the boats, Kennedy decided after Ross's return that they would move to Olasana Island, situated close to the bottom of the anchor shaft and only one island removed from the passage. Olasana lies a mile and three-quarters inward from Plum Pudding in a southwesterly direction.

Again the men dragged the plank into the water, and once more Kennedy took the strap of McMahon's kapok in his teeth and towed him. Kennedy was running the risk of leaving a safe island for one occupied by Japanese. They had not noticed any activity around Olasana, however, and they could see that it abounded in coconut palms. In their weariness the water felt good. Even McMahon was hopeful this time that at least they would reach their destination. It took a few hours to make the crossing. The current seemed stronger among the islands than it was in Blackett Strait. After Kennedy and McMahon were ashore on Olasana, the men had trouble working their way to a point on the beach within a few hundred yards of them. Nearing the island, Albert had left the plank and swum ahead. When he called back to the others they were furious because they feared his voice might be heard by Japanese.

The eleven survivors gathered in the trees behind the curved beach on the southeastern tip of Olasana, whence they could

look straight across another half-mile of water to Naru Island
bordering Ferguson Passage. They talked the situation over, this
time in hushed voices, and asked themselves whether they
should explore Olasana. It appeared about twice the size of
Plum Pudding. "Why go looking for trouble?" someone
inquired. This logic was accepted, and none of them ever saw
more than a corner of the island about fifty yards square. They
gathered coconuts but after eating them, some of the men,
Kennedy and McMahon among them, became ill. Partly as a
joke Ross ate a live snail, which tasted terrible. One of the men
caught a land crab, but no one was hungry enough yet for that.
He tossed it back on the beach. Zinser tried digging for fresh
water, only to split his fingernails on coral. He worried that the
Navy would report him missing in action and subject his wife to
the anguish of fearing he was dead.

By dark all were weary from the long swim. For the first time
in three nights no one went into Ferguson Passage. For the first
time in three nights the boats came through Ferguson Passage
and were on station in Blackett Strait by 9:30 P.M.

The men huddled together in the darkness for warmth.
Though the days were hot, the nights were cool if one had to
sleep in skivvies or in clothing still damp from swimming. The
rumble of the surf on the reef was closer now, and the wind
evoked strange noises in the jungle island. Some of the sounds
difficult to identify caused great anxiety among the men. For
all they knew, they were sharing the island with enemy sen-
tries. An unearthly squeaking sound frightened them until they
deduced that it was made by two branches rubbing together in
the wind. Albert felt lost and asked to sleep next to Ross, whom
he knew the best.

During the night there was a shower. McMahon, his lips
parched, got up to lick some leaves. As he was moving through
the dark, he saw a sight that turned him to marble. Facing him
twenty feet away was the silhouette of a stocky man standing

absolutely still. McMahon froze. He could imagine almond-shaped eyes in a broad face staring at him. He did not know what to do. On his burned feet he could not outrun the man. If he sought concealment on the ground, he could be pounced upon. He had no pistol, no knife. He was afraid to cry out. He just stood motionless, staring. More than anything else, it was the long lapse of time that the two stood facing each other that brought to McMahon the realization that the man could not have been an armed Japanese. Otherwise he would have acted. As suddenly as he had seen him, McMahon recognized Maguire, who was as paralyzed as he was to encounter a figure in the night. The thought had never left Maguire's mind that somewhere during the last three days the Japanese had seen them and sooner or later would turn up to settle accounts.

Although Thursday, August 5, was a day of gratification for the Allied forces because Munda fell, it dawned bleakly for the castaways on Olasana Island. This was the fourth day of their ordeal. The longer they remained in these islands the greater was the danger they would be found by the Japanese. Yet they had no solution to their problem, and the fear of disaster was growing among many of them. On the previous day when someone had moaned that they were all going to die, Johnston had retorted, "Aw, shut up. You can't die. Only the good die young." Now he was not so sure. Nodding to the rosary around Maguire's neck, he said, "Give that necklace a working over." Maguire said that he had often heard that group prayer was effective in certain circumstances. Perhaps they ought to pray together. Thom thought this would be hypocritical. Since many of them did not pray ordinarily, he said, it would not be dignified to make a display of praying now simply because they were in trouble.

If PT 109 was only a sad memory for its crew, it was still a preoccupation of Lt. Evans and his coastwatcher associates. At 9:40 A.M. he messaged KEN:

SIMILAR OBJECT NOW IN FERGUSON PASSAGE DRIFTING
SOUTH X POSITION HALF MILE SE GROSS IS X CANNOT BE
INVESTIGATED FROM HERE FOR AT LEAST TWENTY-FOUR
HOURS

A couple of hours later he informed KEN:

NOW CERTAIN OBJECT IS FOREPART OF SMALL VESSEL X NOW
ON REEF SOUTH GROSS IS

And still later:

HULK STILL ON REEF BUT EXPECT WILL MOVE WITH TONIGHTS
TIDE X DESTRUCTION FROM THIS END NOW MOST UNLIKELY
X IN PRESENT POSITION NO CANOES COULD APPROACH
THROUGH SURF

Kennedy went down the beach a short distance from the
men and beckoned Thom and Ross. "What do we do now?" he
asked them. They had swum into Ferguson Passage at night.
They had changed islands. They had posted lookouts for boats
or planes. Was there anything more they could do to help
themselves? Kennedy was restless. He did not want just to sit
in the shade all day. To keep up the morale of the men, if for
no other reason, they must do something that at least would
give the appearance of striving for a way out. He looked across
to Naru Island. It was only a half-mile swim. The far side of it
faced Ferguson Passage, but what of that? No Allied vessels
would be operating there in daylight. Kennedy had no scheme
into which a visit to Naru fitted. But more or less on the spur
of the moment he said to Ross, "Let's take a look at this one
anyway."

At practically the same time Biuku Gasa and Eroni Kumana
got into their canoe on Wana Wana Island to cross Ferguson Pas-

sage and head back up Blackett Strait to return to their station on Sepo Island. After making their report to Evans the previous day, they had left Kolombangara and passed the night at the native village of Raramana on Wana Wana. Now, after taking leave of friends there, they started paddling on the most direct route to Sepo, which would take them close by Naru, opposite Ferguson Passage from Raramana.

Compared with their earlier swims Kennedy and Ross found the crossing to Naru easy. It was shortly after noon when they crawled up on the white beach of the narrow, four-hundred-yard-long island at the base of the anchor. Black butterflies flitted about the heavy foliage. The ground was pockmarked with crab holes. Thunder from the reefs echoed through the tall palms and casuarina. Kennedy and Ross crept cautiously toward the Ferguson Passage side. Of all the islands in the group, this would be the most logical one for the Japanese to man because of its outlook on the passage. Moreover, just before Kennedy and Ross had left Olasana they had seen some New Zealand P-40s make a strafing attack on the Ferguson Passage side of Naru. They feared that the target of this attack might have been a Japanese outpost and so they moved very carefully through the bushes on Naru.

The distance across the island is short, and they reached the Ferguson shore quickly. Looking out from the fringe of trees, they could see Rendova Peak in its full outline. It was still nearly thirty-eight miles away, but across open water and low islands it looked exasperatingly accessible. Certainly there must be some way, they thought, for eleven men to get to it.

They started along the beach to their left. On the reef about a mile or so from the shore they spied the wreckage of a small Japanese vessel, which is probably what the P-40s had been strafing, and a short distance farther they came upon what appeared to be cargo washed ashore. With the greedy curiosity of a couple of beachcombers they ripped open a rope-bound crate, which to their delight contained hard candy in the shape of tear drops. For a few moments it was like Christmas morning on Naru Island. Briefly, the troubles of war and shipwreck faded. Sucking on hard candy, the two moved on in higher spirits, and Kennedy said that after their exploration was over they would take the candy back to the men. This manna alone would have made the trip to Naru a smashing success. Ross wondered how two swimmers were going to get a crate of candy across a half-mile of salt water.

They had barely gone another twenty yards when they found a dugout canoe that someone had left in the bushes with a large tin of rainwater. Without knowing it they had come upon one of the caches the native scouts had scattered among the islands. They sat down by the canoe and sparingly drank some of the water.

As Biuku and Eroni neared the Naru side of Ferguson Passage they too noticed the Japanese wreckage on the reef and decided to see whether it contained anything of interest. Reaching the reef they anchored their canoe a short distance away and climbed into the hulk. While Kennedy and Ross were quenching their thirst with a can of rainwater, Biuku and Eroni were satisfying their own curiosity by poking through the gear, charts and utensils of one sort and another that were strewn about the deck. The only booty that interested them was Japanese rifles. They each took one and stepped back down on the reef just as Kennedy and Ross re-emerged on the beach.

Across a mile of water both pairs of men instantly spotted one another. Eroni and Biuku, terrified that the two on the beach were Japanese stranded by the wreck and might shoot them, splashed along the reef and tumbled into the canoe, Eroni in his haste dropping his rifle. Kennedy and Ross, thoroughly alarmed that they had been sighted at last by the Japanese, dived into the bushes. Who were those men? Had they actually seen Kennedy and Ross? Would the Japanese garrison soon be alerted to search the islands? The trip to Naru that had begun so auspiciously was now filled with dismaying possibilities.

Eroni and Biuku paddled furiously away from Naru toward Blackett Strait. Once they had rounded the sandbar of Leorava they were headed in the direction of Sepo Island and away from the eleven Americans. If they had just kept going, they would have reached their headquarters several miles away and perhaps forgotten all about the two figures on Naru. At that moment their only interest in the two men was to get away from them and their only mission was to return to Sepo. Had they kept going as they were for just a short distance farther, eleven men on a small Pacific island might never have been heard from again. But at the last moment, they veered clear off their course and headed for Olasana Island.

Biuku had become thirsty from the exertions of their sprint from Naru and persuaded Eroni, who was paddling in the stern, to turn in to Olasana for coconuts. So they took a sharp turn to the left and paddled for the closest point of Olasana, which was the beach at the southeastern tip of the island.

When Kennedy had departed for Naru with Ross he left Thom in charge of the other men. All nine were resting in the bushes behind the beach waiting to hear what the skipper had found on the other island when almost simultaneously three or four of them saw the canoe approaching with the two natives. The men were stunned. After all they had been through, was capture to be their fate? Capture and perhaps torture and finally death? Everyone started to whisper at once. These strangers looked like boys. Perhaps they were scouts for the Japanese on Gizo. If not, there was still no basis on which the men could safely assume that the natives would be friendly. The Americans still had time to fire on them or to slip deeper into the jungle. They probably could avoid detection even now. Biuku and Eroni might get their drink and be off again without seeing them.

At this point, however, Thom made a fateful decision. In a

gamble that involved all their lives he stood up and walked out
on the beach in sight of the strangers, who were now within
thirty feet of the shore.

The sudden apparition of the tattered and bedraggled giant
with the blond beard astounded Biuku and Eroni. Nothing in
their experience had prepared them for the sight of such a
man. In sheer fright they back-paddled as fast as their arms
would go. Thom ran out to the water's edge and beckoned
them with his right hand. "Come, come," he called. Fearful
again that they had happened upon Japanese, the natives
turned their canoe about, thereby bringing a crisis for the
Americans. Self-preservation itself might demand that these
men be stopped, with bullets if necessary, from going off and
possibly reporting their presence to the Japanese. But if the
bullets failed to halt them, the very act of firing would arouse
their hostility and might provoke them into reporting them.
And, either way, the flight of the natives might end the only
chance of rescue.

"Navy, Navy," Thom pleaded. "Americans, Americans."

Eroni and Biuku were a sufficiently safe distance away to
pause and listen. The trouble was they didn't understand what
Thom was saying. Sensing their doubts, he said, "Me no Jap" and
rolled up his right sleeve and showed them his white skin. Biuku
and Eroni still remained dubious. Thom tried another tack. "Me
know Johnny Kari," he said. John Kari was the headman at Wana
Wana, who was known to the PT men through his visits to Lumberi as a native scout. Still no response from Biuku and Eroni.
Then Thom got an inspiration.

"White star," he said, pointing to the sky. "White star."

At last Biuku and Eroni understood. Now they were reas-
sured that Thom and the men who were emerging from the
trees behind him were allies. Slowly the two natives paddled
ashore. The insigne on American aircraft was a white star set in
a white bar. The coastwatchers instructed their native scouts that

airmen who crashed or parachuted from planes bearing the white star were to be treated well and brought with all possible haste to a coastwatcher's station.

The survivors helped Biuku and Eroni drag their canoe across the narrow beach and conceal it between two palm trees. When they all gathered together in the bushes, the meeting was awkward, because the natives were uncomprehending and shy, and few of the sailors really trusted them. Little by little the Americans learned to communicate with Biuku and Eroni. When they understood what the two were trying to say they were shocked. The natives pointed to Naru and indicated the island contained Japanese—meaning Kennedy and Ross. This filled the men with grim doubts as to whether they would ever see the two officers again.

Actually, circumstances were finally taking a more favorable turn for them. That afternoon Evans messaged KEN:

ANTICIPATE MOVING TOMORROW X FINAL ADVICE AM

Evans had come to the conclusion that from Kolombangara he was not getting a good enough view of things in Ferguson Passage and the west side of Blackett Strait. He needed to be more in the center of the area. He passed the word among his scouts, therefore, that the next day he planned to move to a new station on Gomu, one of several smaller islands north of Wana Wana in lower Blackett Strait about seven miles east of Naru, or, as it was also known to Evans, Gross Island. That same afternoon of August 5 he received an advisory from PWD:

AIRINTEL ADVISE THAT HULK WAS EXAMINED BY PLANE TODAY AND WAS THAT BADLY DAMAGED THAT IT WAS NOT WORTH WASTING AMMUNITION

This was the last that was ever known of PT 109.

AFTER A LONG and apprehensive wait in the bushes, Kennedy and Ross, seeing no further signs of the two men in the canoe, resumed their exploration of Naru without making any more discoveries. With the canoe that they had found in the bushes earlier Kennedy now felt much more mobile. He decided to venture out into Ferguson Passage that night, believing he would have a better chance of intercepting the PT boats in a canoe than if he were swimming.

While it was still light, however, he wanted to take the candy and water back to the men on Olasana. He tore a slat off the crate for a paddle and suggested that Ross wait for him. When he left, Ross fell asleep on the beach.

Thom's men also had a canoe now, and they had a long discussion of how they might use it to save themselves. Thom finally decided that he and Starkey and one of the natives would try paddling all the way to Rendova Harbor to organize a rescue party. It would be a long, hard paddle, but the trip seemed perfectly feasible otherwise. When the idea was conveyed to the natives they shook their heads in dissent. Thom was insistent, however, and the natives did not put up any resistance. Biuku got into the canoe with Thom and Starkey. It was not until they were outside the protection of Naru that the two Americans realized that a heavy sea was running in Ferguson Passage. The waves rocked the canoe dangerously. Biuku protested and wanted to return to Olasana. Thom and Starkey nevertheless pushed stubbornly on until they too could see that the canoe would capsize long before they ever reached Rendova. Reluctantly they returned to the island.

At about the same time Kennedy arrived from Naru, to the inexpressible relief of the men. He was surprised to find the two natives, not realizing, of course, that these were the same two men he and Ross had seen. And he was at a loss to know why Biuku and Eroni should be so certain that there were Japanese on Naru.

The only thing Japanese he had found on the island was wreckage and candy, and proceeded to distribute the candy among the nine ravenous men. He also took the tin of water out of the canoe and left it with them before rejoining Ross for the paddle into Ferguson Passage. His hopes would have been high indeed if he could have known that Warfield had ordered the boats through Ferguson Passage that night to patrol in Blackett Strait.

From the outset, however, Kennedy and Ross were in difficulty. The waves that had turned Thom, Starkey and Biuku back were now smashing over the reef, and the wind was rising. Ross thought it foolhardy to pit a canoe against such weather at night and said so. "Barney, I think we ought to go on," Kennedy replied. Once beyond the reef the sea ran too high for them. With slats for paddles they could not keep the bow into the waves. Water splashed over the gunwales. In the stern Ross tried bailing with a coconut shell, but more water poured into the canoe. As they were shouting to each other about turning back a five-foot wave capsized them. They splashed about in the dark until they got a grip on the overturned canoe.

"Sorry I got you out here, Barney," Kennedy called.

"This would be a great time to say I told you so, but I won't," Ross answered.

Spun around by the foaming water, they found their sense of direction confused, but they could see the dark outline of an island, and worked toward it. The reef, when they returned to it, blocked their progress at first, as they swung back and forth in the waves that piled up against the barrier. The swings grew higher and higher until finally Kennedy, Ross, the canoe and tons of water were hurled across the reef in the air. From the deep channel they crashed painfully into shallows jagged with coral. Kennedy lost Ross in the blackness. "Barney," he called. No answer came back. Pierced by the thought that he was responsible for Ross's predicament, he yelled at the top of his lungs, "Barney!" "I'm over here," Ross answered. The canoe had survived the crash intact, and the slats were floating near them.

(Dugout canoes are thick, sturdy craft, hewn with an adze from the trunk of a single tree, preferably a goliti tree. When the natives set out to make a canoe they put a coconut on a stick nearby, and traditionally the job is supposed to be finished when the coconut sprouts in two months.)

On lacerated feet Kennedy and Ross made their way ashore on Naru, sometimes holding the slats down to walk on over rough coral. When they reached the beach they lay down in exhaustion and slept.

The PT boats rolled through the heavy sea and were on station in Blackett Strait at 9:15.

TEN

ON FRIDAY, AUGUST 6, a new animation and earnestness crept into the affairs of the Americans. No great plans had been hatched or master strokes of strategy devised. Nevertheless Kennedy on Naru and his men on Olasana were beginning to feel strongly that they could now do something to help themselves. They had two canoes, and the natives were still with them, having remained overnight on Olasana and built them a fire by rubbing sticks together. Some of the men, as mistrustful as ever, had only pretended to sleep when Biuku and Eroni turned in with them. All night long they had kept a suspicious watch over the natives. The new spirit of the morning was somewhat marred by bad feelings among the survivors because during the night one of them had surreptitiously drunk all the water remaining in the tin.

Despite the battering in Ferguson Passage the night before, Kennedy had been up early and paddled back to his men on Olasana before Ross awoke. When Ross sat up in the sand he was not surprised to find him gone. Kennedy was always on the move, always going somewhere. With his deep-set eyes and black beard Barney Ross looked like Abe Lincoln in Melanesia. All things considered, he was not feeling badly. He was worried, but for five days fear had been a constant companion, and he had learned to live with it.

He swam over to join the others on Olasana and they all sat around talking about how they could best put the canoes and the natives to their service. Kennedy and Thom did not share the suspicions of the men. They were confident that the natives could be trusted.

WHILE THEY were talking, Lt. Evans at 11:10 A.M. radioed KEN:

CLOSING DOWN AT TWO PM AND WILL COMMUNICATE EARLY TOMORROW

With that he gathered his weapons and gear from his hut and trekked down the hillside on Kolombangara with some natives to wait at the shore until dusk when he would paddle to Gomu.

STILL WITHOUT A DEFINITE PLAN of action, Kennedy persuaded Biuku by animated sign language to paddle him back to Naru for another look at Ferguson Passage. Unable to communicate in any but the most rudimentary way with his new ally, Kennedy knew nothing about Evans. As he looked across the passage and the distant flat islands and saw Rendova Peak, he decided that the only practical way to get help would be to send Biuku and Eroni all the way to Lumberi with a message.

He pointed to Rendova Peak and said to Biuku, "Rendova, Rendova." Biuku nodded. "Come here," Kennedy said and led Biuku back into a clearing roofed by towering palms. Kennedy picked up a coconut and had Biuku quarter it. By sticking a sharpened peg in the ground and splitting a coconut on it, the natives know how to husk a coconut in about a tenth of the time it takes an inexperienced white man. Kennedy took his sheath knife and on a polished quarter of the coconut he inscribed the following message to the PT base commander:

NAURO ISL

NATIVE KNOWS POSIT

HE CAN PILOT   11 ALIVE NEED

SMALL BOAT

KENNEDY[†]

Thom, who was still on Olasana with the men, had hit upon the same idea. However, he did not require a coconut because Maguire had the stub of a pencil in his pocket and had somewhere picked up an invoice blank, No. 2860, of the prewar Gizo branch office of Burns Philp (South Sea) Company, Limited. On the back of the invoice Thom wrote this message:

To: Commanding Officer—Oak o
From: Crew P.T. 109 (Oak 14)
Subject: Rescue of 11 (eleven) men lost since Sunday, Aug 1st in enemy action. Native knows our position & will bring P.T. boat back to small islands of Ferguson Passage off NURU IS.

A small boat (outboard or oars) is needed to take men off as some are seriously burned
Signal at night—three dashes (— — —)
Password—Roger—Answer—Wilco

If attempted at day time—advise air coverage or a PBY could set down. Please work out suitable plan & act immediately Help is urgent & in sore need.

Rely on native boys to any extent

L I Thom
Ens. U.S.N.R.
Exec 109

[†]The coconut shell, encased in plastic, currently reposes on President Kennedy's desk in the White House. Thom's widow has his original message on the Burns Philp invoice, which she showed me.

When Kennedy returned to Olasana both messages were
entrusted to Biuku and Eroni, who regarded themselves as being
as much a part of the Allied forces as Kennedy, Evans or anyone
else. With a strong sense of responsibility they embarked for
Rendova Harbor thirty-eight miles away. They first stopped
in Raramana, where they told Benjamin Kevu, the English-
speaking scout, about the survivors. Benjamin, knowing Evans
was on the move, dispatched another scout to Gomu Island to
wait for him and give him the news. From Raramana, Biuku
and Eroni went on foot to the village of Madou, also on Wana
Wana where they picked up John Kari for an overnight paddle
to Rendova Harbor.

Evans meanwhile had arrived at Gomu at nightfall and
received the verbal message from the scout about the eleven
Americans. There was nothing he could do about them immediately. As he had to get his new headquarters set up, he did not
transmit any messages that evening. He decided, however, that
he would send some of his scouts in a large canoe to Naru in the
morning, and that night he penciled a message for them to
carry. It read:

On His Majesty's Service
To Senior Officer, Naru Is.

Friday 11 p.m. Have just learnt of your presence on
Naru Is. & also that two natives have taken news to Rendova. I strongly advise you return immediately to here in
this canoe & by the time you arrive here I will be in Radio
communication with authorities at Rendova & we can
finalise plans to collect balance your party.

A R Evans Lt
R A N V R

Will warn aviation of your crossing Ferguson Passage

Early on Saturday morning, August 7, Biuku, Eroni and John Kari reached Blanche Channel. The Navy had a base at Roviana Island, near Munda, and as this was closer than Rendova the three natives stopped there and showed Kennedy's coconut shell and Thom's letter to an officer. He immediately ordered a whaleboat to take them to the base at Sasavele Island farther down the New Georgia coast, whence they were whisked over to Rendova Harbor in a PT boat. Lumberi was already in a state of excitement over a message that had just been relayed from Evans. At 9:20 A.M. he had radioed KEN:

ELEVEN SURVIVORS PT BOAT ON GROSS IS X HAVE SENT FOOD AND LETTER ADVISING SENIOR COME HERE WITHOUT DELAY X WARN AVIATION OF CANOES CROSSING FERGUSON

At 11:30 A.M. PWD messaged Evans:

GREAT NEWS X COMMANDER PT BASE RECEIVED A MESSAGE JUST AFTER YOURS FROM SURVIVORS BY NATIVE X THEY GAVE THEIR POSITION AND NEWS THAT SOME ARE BADLY WOUNDED AND REQUEST RESCUE X WE PASSED THE NEWS THAT YOU HAD SENT CANOES AND WITHOUT WISHING TO INTERFERE WITH YOUR ARRANGEMENTS WANT TO KNOW CAN THEY ASSIST X[†] THEY WOULD SEND SURFACE CRAFT TO MEET YOUR RETURNING CANOES OR ANYTHING YOU ADVISE X THEY WISH TO EXPRESS GREAT APPRECIATION X WE WILL AWAIT YOUR ADVICE AND PASS ON

At 12:45 P.M. Evans replied:

COULD ONLY MAN ONE CANOE SUITABLE FOR CROSSING X NO SIGN ITS RETURN YET X GO AHEAD AND SEND SURFACE

[†]The meaning of this sentence is that the PT officers at Lumberi wanted to know if they could assist Evans in any way.

CRAFT WITH SUITABLE RAFT OR DINGHIES X IF ANY ARRIVE
HERE LATER WILL SEND OTHER ROUTE X PLEASE KEEP ME
INFORMED

Evans sent seven of his scouts for Kennedy—Moses Sesa,
Jonathan Bia, Joseph Eta, Stephen Hitu, Koete Igolo, Edward
Kidoe and Benjamin Kevu, who was the leader.[†] From the
information passed on by Biuku and Eroni on their way back to
Rendova the seven knew that the Americans were on Olasana
Island but they did not know what part. After a paddle of more
than two hours they glided up on a beach without seeing a sign
of any survivors. They listened but heard nothing. Dividing into
two groups, one circled the island to the right, the other to the
left. In the group that was headed to the left Moses Sesa
motioned to the men to stop. Footprints ran across into the
underbrush. Cautious at first because of the presence of Japanese
in the region, the natives followed the footprints to a clearing
where they discovered the survivors.

Everything about the arrival of Evans's scouts on Olasana
Island seemed unbelievable.

Kennedy, who had barely smiled in a week, was tickled
when handed a communication beginning, "On His Majesty's
Service," by a black man naked except for a cloth around his
waist. Here he was, bearded, gaunt, unwashed, half-starved,
half-naked, blotched with festering coral wounds, castaway on
a miserable patch of jungle surrounded by sharks, being
greeted as if he were in his father's embassy in London.

"You've got to hand it to the British," he said to Ross.

The canoe itself was a cornucopia. Before the gluttonous eyes

---

[†]These seven, as well as Biuku Gasa, Eroni Kumana and John Kari, are alive and
in good health in the Solomon Islands today and remember as one of the great
moments of their lives the rescue of "Captain Kennedy" and the crew of his PT
boat. The event is celebrated in a folk song that has been sung in the islands for
years.

of eleven famished sailors, yams, pawpaws, rice, potatoes, boiled fish, Chelsea cigarettes and C rations with roast-beef hash poured ashore. Some of the natives scampered up palm trees like monkeys to fetch coconuts. Others collected palm fronds and built a hut for McMahon. Still others lighted three kerosene burners for cooking. His idle period at an end, Mauer stepped in to raise the hash above the level of a C ration. The natives fashioned dishes out of coconut shells and spoons out of palm fronds.

Benjamin's command of English shamed some of the sailors. He had learned to read and write at a Methodist mission school, mastering the language sufficiently by 1930 to get a job with the British Solomon Islands Protectorate in Gizo, clerking in the post office and the treasury. He acquired western manners and was a man of marked civility. While in Gizo he married and raised a family. Just before the Japanese invasion, however, the British burned all their facilities and bade the natives work with the coastwatchers. Benjamin paddled his wife and children to Raramana and became a scout.

The sailors invited the natives to eat with them, but they insisted on eating apart by themselves. When the meal was over, Benjamin suggested to Kennedy that it was time to leave for Gomu. It was possible for only one American to be hidden in the canoe with seven natives paddling, and since Evans had urged that the "senior" should come, Kennedy had little choice no matter what reservations he might have about leaving his men.

The natives tossed some dead palm fronds into the canoe to conceal him when they got out into Blackett Strait. Looking ahead to the problems of rescue, Kennedy knew it would be difficult to find an opening in the reef at night. As the canoe passed through the reef into Blackett Strait, therefore, he glanced back to get a point of reference on Olasana that he might be able to recognize in the dark. After he felt that he had the location of the opening fixed in his mind he lay down in the middle of the canoe with his feet toward the bow. Benjamin covered him with fronds and knelt by his head, paddling and occasionally chatting with him.

Half way to Gomu the paddlers heard the hum of airplane engines. First a single Japanese plane flew in from sea and circled over them and then two more enemy planes, from Vila. The natives were frightened that the Japanese somehow knew about their passenger and would destroy them all.

"What's going on?" Kennedy asked through the fronds.

"Japanese planes," Benjamin replied. "Stay down!"

Jonathan Bia wanted Benjamin to make a friendly gesture to the planes, but Benjamin feared this might only make the pilots suspicious.

"Can I look now?" Kennedy inquired.

"No, no, no," Benjamin snapped. "Keep down!"

After an argument with Jonathan, Benjamin stood up and waved at the planes. Jonathan was right. Eventually the Japanese flew away, and the natives, five of them Methodists and two Seventh-Day Adventists, burst into hymns.

Evans meanwhile was watching anxiously from Gomu. When, shortly before 6 P.M., his binoculars picked up the approaching natives, he was dismayed not to see any American in the canoe. Then it dawned on him that of course the natives would have concealed such a passenger. When the canoe touched the sand, Kennedy stuck his head through the palm fronds and smiled at Evans.

"Hello," he said, "I'm Kennedy."

Evans introduced himself,[†] and they shook hands. The coast-

---

[†]In his weariness and excitement Kennedy forgot Evans's name. He kept his letter, but the signature was run together so that A. R. Evans looked for all the world like A. Rinhaus, which for the next seventeen years was the name by which Kennedy remembered the coastwatcher. Evans's identity was further obscured by the Hersey article. Writing during the war while secrecy still surrounded the

watcher was surprised at the youthfulness of his guest and gratified that he was in as good condition as he was.

"Come and have some tea," he invited him.

They walked back from the beach to an old wooden house
on the island. Evans was in shorts. Kennedy was wearing skivvies
and was barefoot. Over tea they discussed rescue plans.

Evans showed Kennedy a message from Lumberi, relayed by
PWD at 1:51 P.M.:

THREE PT BOATS PROCEED TONIGHT AND WILL BE AT GROSS
ISLAND ABOUT TEN PM X THEY WILL TAKE RAFTS ETC X WILL
INFORM YOU WHEN WE RECEIVE ADVICE OF RESCUE

Evans further suggested to Kennedy that the natives paddle
him back to Rendova by way of the Wana Wana Lagoon while
the PT boats went in to pick up the men. Kennedy would not
hear of either plan. It would be difficult, perhaps impossible, for
anyone who did not know exactly where they were to find the
men in the dark, he argued. Moreover, he said, he was responsible for his men, and it was his duty to remain with them until
they were safe. He said he wanted to meet the PT boats on the
way to the islands and go in with them. With the help of Evans's
charts they worked out a superseding plan, which, at 6:50, Evans
radioed to PWD for relay to Lumberi:

LIEUT KENNEDY CONSIDERS IT ADVISABLE THAT HE PILOT PT
BOATS TONIGHT X HE WILL AWAIT BOATS NEAR PATPARAN
ISLAND X PT BOAT TO APPROACH ISLAND FROM NW TEN PM
AS CLOSE AS POSSIBLE X BOAT TO FIRE FOUR SHOTS AS

---

coastwatcher organization, Hersey referred to Evans as Lt. Wincote, a New
Zealand infantry officer. It was not until after Kennedy became President that
the discovery was made in Australia that Reg Evans, a modest accountant in Sydney, was the coastwatcher whose scouts had found Kennedy and his men and who
had helped organize the rescue.

RECOGNITION X HE WILL ACKNOWLEDGE WITH SAME AND
GO ALONGSIDE IN CANOE X SURVIVORS NOW ON ISLAND
NW OF GROSS X HE ADVISES OUTBOARD MOTOR X PATPARAN
IS ONE AND HALF MILES AND BEARS TWO ONE FOUR DEGREES
FROM MAKUTI

Shortly after eight o'clock the scouts were ready to paddle
Kennedy to Patparan for the rendezvous. It was cool, and he
borrowed a pair of cover-alls from Evans to wear until he was
picked up. Then, just as he was about to leave, he discovered
that he had only three bullets left in his .38, Ross having fired
the others the night he swam into Ferguson Passage. The plan
submitted to Lumberi had specified four shots for recognition,
and it was too late to change it because the boats would already
have left. Kennedy solved the problem by borrowing Evans's
Japanese rifle, promising to leave it in the canoe with the
cover-alls. The two men, whose meeting had come about
through such an improbable chain of circumstances, shook
hands and said good-by without either one having any expec-
tation of ever seeing or hearing of the other again.

It was well after ten when Kennedy finally heard the rumble
of engines and then four shots in the dark northwest of Patparan
Island. He stood up in the canoe and fired three shots with his
revolver, after which he pulled the trigger of the rifle. The kick
nearly knocked him into the water. The natives paddled forward until they glided along the starboard side of Lt. Liebenow's
PT 157.

"Hey, Jack!" a voice called.

"Where the hell have you been?" Kennedy demanded.

"We've got some food for you," someone said.

"Thanks," Kennedy replied, dryly. "I've just had a coconut."

He was hauled aboard with jubilation. Lt. Cluster, commander of Squadron 2, was there. So was Brantingham. So were
the two natives, Biuku and Eroni. So were several newspaper

correspondents. Kennedy tossed the cover-alls back into the canoe, but in the excitement forgot about the rifle.[†]

"THE BOATS ARE HERE!" The shout went up on the beach at Olasana. It was after midnight. The men had been expecting to be rescued. Nevertheless many hours had passed since the natives took Kennedy away in mid-afternoon, and no one knew better than the ten men on the island that accidents frequently altered plans in the Solomons at the height of war. The shouts brought men running—or hobbling—to the shore. McMahon dragged himself from the hut the natives had built for him where he had been sleeping off his first meal in a week. Ross limped on a knee swollen by coral cuts. Thom rushed into the water up to his waist—dubious until he heard a certain accent calling, "Lenny! Hey, Lenny!"

After picking Kennedy up, Liebenow had taken the boat across Ferguson Passage and worked his way along the reef, the arm of the anchor swinging from Naru northward to Plum Pudding. About midway between Leorava and Three Palm Islet Kennedy said there was an opening. When the crew questioned it, he insisted that he had that very afternoon come through an opening there. He scanned the dark off the port side until he was sure he could see the contour of Olasana as he had fixed it in his mind. The others argued with him. The crew, quite naturally, was concerned lest, turning to port, they become stranded on the reef. This was happening all too often to PT boats. If it should happen now it would be a disaster not only for everyone aboard PT 157, but for the men on Olasana, because it would surely bring the Japanese down on all of them at daybreak.

Kennedy said that if he could have a raft he would show them

[†]When Evans visited him in the White House in 1961, President Kennedy apologized for the oversight. The rifle disappeared.

where there was an opening. A rubber raft was lowered over the side, and Biuku and Eroni paddled ahead, probing as they went. PT 157 rumbled slowly behind. In a couple of minutes the boat was safely through the reef. Sure of his position now, Kennedy exultantly called through the dark to Thom. Some of the other officers tried to shush him lest the enemy hear his voice, but he was in no mood to be quiet. "Lenny! Hey, Lenny!" he shouted. A shout came back. Liebenow and the others could hear voices up ahead. The engines were turned off, and a dinghy went in to the island. Presently it returned through the night with a couple of ragged passengers. Within a short time all the survivors of PT 109 were shuttled aboard.

The journey back to Rendova was as bizarre a mission as the United States Navy ever undertook in the South Pacific. As prescribed in the regulations, medical corpsmen gave the survivors brandy, with effects not altogether foreseen by the Surgeon General of the Navy. Having learned, for example, that Biuku and Eroni had attended mission schools, Johnston collared the two of them for endless renditions of

> Jesus loves me, this I know,
> For the Bible tells me so . . .

The ribbing of the men of PT 109 for failing to get out of the way of the Japanese Navy began, even in pidgin English— "What! You one fella Mary because you loosim boat belong you?"[†]

"How are you feeling, Mac?" Lt. Cluster asked McMahon.

"Just fine, thanks, Mr. Cluster," he replied.

The first light of dawn was in the east when PT 157 curved into Rendova Harbor on Sunday, August 8, one week after the men on PT 109 had departed their base. At Todd City John

---

[†]Roughly translated: "Aren't you an old woman for losing your boat?"

Maguire met his brother, Bill, who had been waiting in an agony of suspense. John wanted to hug him, but in the presence of the others he merely shook his hand.

"You didn't write Mom about this, did you?" he asked. Their mother was seriously ill.

"No," Bill replied. "I couldn't bring myself to do it."

The returning castaways were told by the men at the base that a memorial service had been held for them.[†]

Later the telephone rang at Hyannis Port, Massachusetts, and Kennedy's mother answered.

"Jack's been saved!" a friend exclaimed.

"Saved from what?" Mrs. Kennedy asked.

Her husband was down at the riding stables when she told him about the call. For him the impact was much greater. Two or three days earlier he had heard[††] that his son was missing in the South Pacific. He had not been able to bring himself to break the terrible news to his wife.

One year after the sinking of PT 109, on August 12, 1944, Joseph Kennedy received the news that his older son, Joe, Jr., had been reported missing on a bombing mission over the Belgian coast. This time there was no happy ending.

[†] I have been unable to verify that such a service was actually conducted.

[††] After the lapse of eighteen years he cannot recall who told him, but he feels certain that he did not learn it from officials of the government. The crew was never officially reported as missing in action. The rescue was effected in time to prevent this.

ELEVEN

For Lt. John F. Kennedy this was not the end of PT boats or the war in the Pacific. Before the end came, there would be another boat—PT 59—and another extraordinary and dangerous mission. A man would die in Kennedy's bunk, and his boat, overloaded with fifty-five to sixty-five men, would lie quietly in the darkness off an enemy coast beneath enemy guns without enough gas to return to its base.

From their rescue in Blackett Strait, Kennedy and his crew had been brought back to a sick bay in Tulagi Harbor following the brief stop at Lumberi. Before departing Lumberi Kennedy thanked Biuku and Eroni and said he hoped to see them again in the islands after the war. He had a trinket for both of them and, in addition, he gave Biuku his Pacific Theater ribbon.†

---

†Biuku and Eroni display these gifts with pride today. In addition they and the other natives who participated in the rescue have autographed pictures of the President of the United States. The election of Mr. Kennedy caused great interest and definite pride in those remote islands of New Georgia, Gizo, Kolombangara and Wana Wana. The natives know little about the United States and have no understanding of the Presidency. They realize, however, that the young naval officer they rescued is now a headman of great importance in the world. The interisland vessels have radios, and at the docks the natives hear, "President Kennedy this, and President Kennedy that" on the news broadcasts from Honiara, Guadalcanal. The name arrests their attention. They are perfectly well aware that he might not be where he is if it had not been for them.

In the thatched sick bay at Tulagi Harbor he brooded over the fate of PT 109. Though about to be promoted to full lieutenant, though the holder of a Purple Heart and the recipient of the Navy and Marine Corps Medal awarded for his gallantry toward his shipwrecked crew of PT 109, Kennedy did not feel that his career in the South Pacific was anything to write home about. Lt. Cluster reminded him that Navy custom permitted an officer who had been shipwrecked to go home or at least to get another assignment to his liking until transportation home was available. Kennedy replied that he did not want to go home. He had come all the way to the South Pacific, he said, and had not accomplished anything yet. He wanted another boat if he could get one.

Cluster asked him if he would be interested in forming a crew and taking over a PT boat that, as an experiment, was about to be converted into a gunboat as a more formidable weapon against enemy barges. Kennedy was eager for the assignment, and Cluster made him skipper of PT 59. In essence the transformation of the boat would consist of removing the four torpedo tubes and replacing them with additional machine guns behind armor shields. Also, instead of the 20-millimeter anti-aircraft gun on the stem the gunboat would carry 40-millimeter guns fore and aft.

Many of the old crew, of course, had already been shifted. Thom, who also was awarded the Navy and Marine Corps Medal for saving the lives of men on PT 109, was promoted and given a boat of his own.[†] Ross became executive officer on another PT boat.[††] He and Kennedy, who had grown quite close

---

[†]After the war Thom went home and married his college sweetheart, Kate Holway, and they had two children. In 1946 he was selling insurance while working for a master's degree at Ohio State. On October 4, driving from Columbus to his wife's parents' home in Youngstown, where they were living because of the housing shortage, his car was struck by a train near Ravenna, Ohio. He died the next day. Kennedy interrupted his campaign for Representative of the 11th District of Massachusetts to rush to Youngstown.

[††]In 1961 President Kennedy appointed Ross to the staff of the President's Committee on Juvenile Delinquency and Youth Crime.

during their ordeal, would see a good deal of each other in the years to come. McMahon and Johnston were physically unfit for further action.

Albert was reassigned to the crew of Ensign Edward H. Kruse, Jr.,[†] in PT 163 only to be treacherously killed several weeks later. On the night of October 6–7 the Japanese destroyer *Yugumo* was sunk by an American torpedo during the battle of Vella Lavella. The next day PT 163 was ordered to the Slot to pick up some survivors for interrogation. The Japanese sailors submitted to being hauled aboard only when Kruse pointed his guns in their faces. The prisoners were ordered to strip and lie on the foredeck while Albert and another sailor were stationed on either side of the cockpit with sub-machine guns to guard them. At dusk, as PT 163 was nearing its base, a prisoner, the one who had been the toughest to deal with in the water, appealed to Albert for a drink. Twenty, good-hearted and inexperienced, Albert fetched a cup of water and handed it to him. Instead of taking the cup the Japanese grabbed the sub-machine gun slung under Albert's arm. Albert struggled desperately, but the fellow had the jump on him. He forced the barrel against Albert's chest and pulled the trigger. Several prisoners leaped up. It was the last thing that they—and Albert's killer—ever did. The other sailor standing guard with Albert slaughtered every man who was not lying flat on his back.

Of the old PT 109 crew, only Maguire,[††] Mauer, Kowal,[†††] Drewitch and Drawdy were still available. Kennedy told them that after all they had endured he did not feel justified in asking them to rejoin him but he said that he would be happy to

---

[†]Afterward Representative Kruse, Democrat, of Indiana.

[††]In 1961 President Kennedy appointed Maguire United States Marshal for the Southern District of Florida.

[†††]In 1961 President Kennedy promulgated an executive order clearing the way for Kowal's appointment to the National Park Service.

have them aboard PT 59. All of them volunteered. In time the PT 59 roster of enlisted men lengthened with such new names as Helmer, Christianson, Cline, Alexander, Servatius, Slagle, Scribner, Strickland and Facto.

As his executive officer Kennedy chose Lt. (jg) Robert Lee Rhoads, Jr., a lean alert professional at twenty-one, who had been on the point of completing his course at the California Maritime Academy when the Japanese attacked Pearl Harbor. He was appointed an ensign in the Navy in June 1942 and was the navigator of the Liberty ship *Aludra* when she was sunk by a Japanese submarine between Guadalcanal and San Cristobal on June 23, 1943. The destroyer *Skylark* picked up the lifeboat he was in and took him to Espiritu Santo. From there he was transferred to Nouméa, volunteered for PT boats and sent to Sesape.

Kennedy and Rhoads reported aboard on September 1. It took more than a month for workers on a repair ship to reconvert PT 59. While most of the boat's crew amused themselves with such familiar Sesape pastimes as listening to Tokyo Rose, swapping Spam with the natives for bananas, and scrounging for alky, Kennedy and Rhoads lived aboard the repair ship. Having nothing to do while workmen were taking their boat apart, both were tapped as censors. Sitting in the ward room every night reading outgoing mail made Kennedy so restless that he finally concocted some meaningless chore for himself and Rhoads in connection with the refitting.

One day they rowed ashore with a sample of the armor plate being installed on PT 59. Dragging it to a range, they fired .30- and .50-caliber machine guns at it. On frontal fire the bullets made Swiss cheese of the thing. Kennedy shrugged. Rhoads looked unhappy. There was nothing they could do about it. At least, they agreed, it might be helpful against bullets coming in at an angle or fired from a great distance.

The refitting was completed on October 7. After the bottom was painted and the propellers and shafts replaced, Kennedy hit

the old trail to the Russells again. They spent one night near
the scenes of the alligator hunts and the fuel dock and tool shed,
now repaired from the slice of PT 109's bow, and then continued to Rendova Harbor on October 10. On the way one of
the new men passed the time off watch shooting at seagulls with
a .45. Seeing the results, the rest of the crew hoped that he
would not be assigned as a gunner. To Kennedy and the old crew
the last mile of Blanche Channel was like returning to a place
they had known all their lives. A great many more ships were
in Rendova Harbor now than when they had first seen it three
months before, and the expanded facilities of Lumberi had
spilled over to Bau Island.

Kennedy remained at Rendova for a week, getting his boat
and his crew in shape for combat. On October 11 they tossed
some empty oil drums into the sea and made firing runs
on them to test the guns and enable the skipper to decide
who should man them. The next day they found they had to
replace the center screw. They made a cruise for compass-
compensating and had a few more runs at floating oil drums.
At 1:15 P.M. on October 18 they left. They cut through Ferguson
Passage and Blackett Strait passing by Naru, Olasana, Plum Pudding, Gizo, Kolombangara and other familiar landmarks. At 4:30,
after crossing Vella Gulf, they cruised into Lambu Lambu Cove,
where Kennedy reported to Lt. Berndtson, recently shifted from
executive officer at Lumberi to base commander at Lambu Lambu.

Berndtson had been born to the sea. His grandfather was a
yacht captain in Sweden and frequently took the King on
cruises. His father went to sea at fourteen, served in the United
States Navy in World War I and became the first captain of the
Lurline, the luxurious Matson liner that sails between California and Hawaii. Young Arthur went from Oakland High School
to Annapolis, where he was graduated in the Class of '40. At
first he was a gunnery division officer on the *Enterprise*. Then,
after taking part in the invasion of Guadalcanal, he was sent to

Melville for training as a PT officer and then back to the Solomons. In the meanwhile the *Lurline*, with his father still skipper, became a transport, and the Berndtsons' paths crossed several times in the South Pacific.

There was not a great deal for Berndtson to show Kennedy at Lambu Lambu. The cove, a couple of hundred yards wide at the mouth, lies on the north coast of Vella Lavella, opening on the Slot. The distance directly across to the central part of Choiseul is thirty-five miles, but it is roughly sixty-five miles from Lambu Lambu to the Warrior River and Choiseul Bay area, which lies at the upper end of Choiseul Island. The natives say that the Slot between Vella Lavella and Choiseul is inhabited by sea devils, who approach ships sometimes in the guise of white lights and disappear in a burst of colors when they are just off the starboard side.

After the fall of Munda the Solomon Islands began slipping out of Japan's grasp. The scene of action moved up a tier from the New Georgia–Gizo–Kolombangara triangle to the triangle described by Vella Lavella, Choiseul and Bougainville. The Allies landed on Vella Lavella on August 15, and the Japanese finally evacuated the island in the first week of October, after which the build-up for the invasion of Bougainville got under way.

Before the war Lambu Lambu had been a small Chinese trading post with a single thatched hut on stilts. The PT base, which Berndtson ran on a shoestring, was scarcely more imposing. Except for the dock there was no installation in the cove to speak of. LSTs would put in and toss fuel drums up on the shore, whence sailors would have to roll them by brute force over the tangle of mangrove roots to the dock. Flies and mosquitoes were a plague. Food was scarce. The heat was heavy with tropical showers that kept everything mouldy and musty. Clothes were never really dry. If Lumberi was a wilderness, Lambu Lambu was little more than a mangrove swamp, where green lizards a foot long glided over damp roots and scorpions dropped out of trees into PT boats moored below.

Lambu Lambu Cove leads back into a small river, which is known to the natives as the Katapaqu but which could as suitably be called the Styx. It is a dark, fetid stream that flows through blackened mangrove roots into heavy jungle and looks as though it may disappear eventually into a dismal cavern. The screech of strange birds pierces the foliage. At night wild dogs howl. It was believed that these dogs could detect approaching aircraft sooner than man or mechanism.

PT 59 was a seventy-seven-foot Elco, older than PT 109 and with even scantier accommodations. Those who were lucky enough to have jungle hammocks slept in them. The others slept in tents, connected with the moored boats by catwalks thrown over the rat-infested mangrove roots. Sailors who removed their shoes at night were as likely as not to find them tenanted by land crabs the next morning—and the discovery was usually made with the toes.

On his rounds of the new base Kennedy met an old friend. Berndtson's intelligence officer was Lt. (jg) Byron R. ("Whizzer") White,† the former University of Colorado halfback and All-American whom Kennedy had met in London when White was a Rhodes scholar and later on the Continent. One night White went out on patrol with Kennedy, tried his hand at a machine gun and received a gash in the palm from a malfunctioning bolt.

At Vella Lavella Kennedy was sent out on patrol as often as at Rendova. On October 18, the very day PT 59 arrived at the new base, he was patrolling with PT 169 and PT 183 off the northwestern tip of Choiseul. Their mission, in part, was to block the western and southern approaches to Choiseul Bay, an important base for Japanese barges. A half-hour after midnight, when

---

† In 1961 President Kennedy appointed White Deputy Attorney General.

the three boats were five miles south of Redman Island, a single-engine Japanese plane winged across their path and dropped two bombs, which crashed into the water off the starboard side of PT 59. Kennedy shouted, "Commence firing," but his gunners failed to bring down the attacker.

After scanning the Emerald Entrance (so called on the maps) to Choiseul Bay, the boats turned southward to the Warrior River, a stream that winds down the western slope of Choiseul and empties into the Slot at Salovai Harbor. It is doubtful that Kennedy or his men prior to this mission had ever heard of the Warrior River, but before many days were to pass they would hear of it again—and they would never forget it.

A half-mile off the river's mouth the radar carried by Kennedy's new boat picked up two planes a couple of miles to seaward. "General quarters!" the skipper called, but the planes soon disappeared. On the way back to Lambu Lambu Cove, however, the boats were attacked again by a lone enemy aircraft. The pilot dropped a bomb in their midst and then circled about for a second run. This time two white holes were torn in the black sea around them. As a gunboat PT 59 carried considerably more armament than other PTs. Kennedy's crew opened fire with two 40-millimeter anti-aircraft guns as well as with .30- and .50-caliber machine guns. Still, the fight was a stand-off. The plane escaped to the north, and the three boats returned undamaged to Lambu Lambu.

"Were you scared?" Kennedy asked Rhoads.

"Hell, yes," he said.

"So was I," Kennedy admitted.

On the night of October 20–21, PT 59 departed Lambu Lambu at seven o'clock. Twenty miles out the crew saw the overcast turn red from a flare. No plane appeared, and the boat sped on to Choiseul Bay, skirting the islands outside the harbor. That night Kennedy went as far north as Poroporo and West Cape. On the night of October 21–22 he was off Choiseul

Bay again for an uneventful patrol in squally weather. Returning from these patrols at dawn the men observed that on one of the small islands in the Slot the Japanese had built a privy over the water. The first time they saw it they asked Kennedy if they might fire on it. "No," he replied. The second time they repeated the request, but again he said emphatically that ammunition had not been shipped all the way to Vella Lavella to be expended on latrines. The target was so tempting, however, that their request became chronic. On October 26, PT 59 was back off Choiseul in a patrol that was bombed but not damaged by enemy planes.

On October 27 the 2nd Marine Parachute Battalion invaded Choiseul by sea. The Choiseul diversion, as the operation was known, was a hazardous affair throughout. Commanded by Lt. Colonel Victor H. Krulak, the battalion landed at Voza on the southwest coast of Choiseul opposite Vella Lavella. It moved into the hilly jungle island in the thick of numerous Japanese forces. Serving as a mask for the Allies' true intention of launching a major invasion of Bougainville, its mission was to seem to be more than it was. The business of making a battalion-sized landing look like the main Allied thrust in the northern Solomons naturally took a good deal of spreading out and moving noisily about. Thus it happened that on November 1 a reconnaissance patrol of eighty-seven Marines, almost all of them from Company G, was ordered up the coast to attack enemy troops along the way and ultimately to lob mortar shells into Japanese installations in Choiseul Bay.

A few days before the landing a Marine officer-messenger in battle dress had sped down one of the dirt roads of Vella Lavella in a jeep and, wheeling into the PT base at Lambu Lambu, handed a sealed envelope to Lt. Berndtson. In the envelope was a top-secret message notifying him that the 2nd Marine Parachute Battalion stationed on Vella Lavella was about to invade Choiseul Island as a diversionary attack. The message listed the PTs at Lambu Lambu as supporting units to be on call in any emergency that might arise.

The eighty-seven-man patrol on Choiseul was commanded by Major Warner T. Bigger, twenty-six, a graduate of the University of Florida, whose father was a naval officer and once sailed in the old frigate *Hartford*, renowned as Admiral David Farragut's flagship at Mobile Bay. Major Bigger had been a Marine officer aboard the cruisers *Helena* and *Louisville* before taking parachute training and was currently the battalion executive officer. Under him was Captain William R. Day, commander of Company G, who was to survive the ordeal of the next twenty-four hours only to be killed on Iwo Jima. The medical officer, for whom there was to be little rest, was Navy Lt. John S. Stevens, twenty-eight, of Bridgeport, Connecticut.

The eighty-seven Marines with two native guides moved up the coast from Voza in two LCPRs (landing craft, personnel, ramp) as far as the Warrior River. When they turned into the river to put the patrol ashore everything started to go wrong. The river, shown on charts as being deep enough for small schooners, was too shallow even for the flatbottom LCPRs. Once through the mouth the boats began to run aground. To clear them the coxswains had to gun the engines. The jungle echoed to the roar, and Bigger was sure that the Japanese must have heard it. He ordered the LCPRs to land him on the east bank and then retire a few miles back up the coast to Nukiki and wait to pick the patrol up late that afternoon. After setting up a base camp on the river bank Bigger pushed inland with the main body of his men. His plan was to reach Choiseul Bay by encircling the bending course of the river.

By mid-afternoon, however, instead of standing beyond the headwaters of the Warrior, as he had anticipated, Bigger was in the middle of a large swamp with his men, struggling along on

the heels of the native guides. When he demanded that they find
him a better route, the guides admitted that they were lost. The
two natives who had been assigned to the patrol lived in a different part of Choiseul and knew no more about the Warrior
River region than Bigger did.

Rather than risk losing part of his patrol in the dark Bigger
decided to make his mission a two-day affair and bivouac overnight in the swamp. He ordered Lt. Rea E. Duncan to return
to the base camp with a squad and notify Krulak by radio what
had happened. Duncan did so and then spent the night not far
from the camp. When he awoke the next morning he discovered
that Japanese troops, perhaps attracted by the roaring motors,
had moved in between him and Bigger, surrounding the camp
and the radio and severing Bigger's line of retreat. Bigger and his
men, however, were still ignorant of their danger.

To get help Duncan slipped away with his squad without
attracting attention. They hastened to Nukiki and embarked in
an LCPR for Voza to tell Krulak of Bigger's danger. Krulak
radioed an urgent call for fighter cover and PT boats to help
evacuate the patrol.

In mid-afternoon on November 2, the message arrived for
Berndtson by radio. It was marked "Urgent" and appealed for
help for the trapped patrol. The essence of it was that the
fate of eighty-seven officers and men depended on the speed
with which PT boats could get to the Warrior River and rescue
them.

Only a few hours of daylight remained. Berndtson ran down
the trail that led from the operations dugout in the bivouac area
to the primitive dock. He tried to recollect what boats he had
available. His entire flotilla, to stretch a word, consisted of five
boats. One, he remembered, was laid up for repairs and would be
useless in such an emergency. Two others he had already ordered
to go out on patrol that night in accordance with his daily
instructions from CTF 31. Two boats were left, therefore, and

Berndtson had no idea whether they were fueled. Nearing the cove he could see that the boat then at the dock refueling was PT 59, one of the unassigned boats. Kennedy, in shorts, khaki shirt and Army fatigue cap, was on the dock with the men who were wrestling oil drums over mangrove roots to the side of his boat.

"Jack, look at this," Berndtson said between breaths. Kennedy scanned the message.

"How much gas have you aboard?" Berndtson asked.

"What have we got on now, Drawdy?" Kennedy called. Drawdy answered, "Seven hundred gallons." The capacity was twenty-two hundred gallons.

"That would get you over," Berndtson said.

"Yes, we could get *over*," Kennedy agreed. The problem was how to get back with the Marines. Seven hundred gallons was not nearly enough for a round trip across the Slot at the high speed that would be required, yet in the circumstances time did not permit hauling more aboard.

On inquiry Berndtson found that the other available boat was fully fueled. Would it be feasible, he asked, for the two boats to go to the rescue of the Marines with the understanding that when Kennedy ran out of fuel after the evacuation, as was certain to happen, the other boat would tow him? One boat alone would not provide space enough for eighty-seven passengers. After talking it over the officers agreed that in this emergency they had to try.

"Get going, then," Berndtson urged.

"Let's go get them," Kennedy said, hopping aboard. "Wind her up!"

Kennedy told his men simply that they were going over to Choiseul to pick up some Marines who were in trouble. He did not know any more about it than that except that his mission was a very urgent one. The message that Berndtson had received from Guadalcanal did not identify the location on

Choiseul where the Marines were trapped. Instead it gave a compass bearing on the Choiseul shore where a guide boat would be awaiting the PTs and would lead them to the encircled Marines. Berndtson marked the point on a chart, which Kennedy handed to Rhoads, who was regarded by all the crew as an excellent navigator.

Nevertheless as they sped out into the Slot at 4:35 P.M. with the other PT boat racing along behind, everyone aboard PT 59 responsible for the success of the mission was worried. Rhoads worried about being able to locate a guide boat sixty-five miles away with nothing more than a compass bearing to go on. Operating within relatively small areas, as they had been doing in the Solomons, the PTs had used their compasses very little. Rhoads wondered how true the compass aboard PT 59 was and wished they had taken better care of it. Drawdy, for whom a steadily falling needle on a gauge was becoming an obsession, stood in the engine room and worried about the dwindling gasoline supply. For all that had happened to them, he reflected, they had never been in a predicament like this before. At the wheel, Kennedy squinting at the hilly Choiseul coast rising ahead worried whether they could find the Marines in time to help them. He wished there were more daylight left.

On Choiseul Island, meanwhile, Bigger and his men were still unaware that Japanese troops had moved in behind them. From their swampy bivouac they had set out at daybreak to complete their mission of shelling the main installations in Choiseul Bay.

As they neared their objective, they saw an enemy outpost. Two Japanese were washing clothes. One was standing guard. A fourth was in a shack. The Marines, creeping up, shot and killed three of them. The fourth escaped. Bigger feared that the sound of the firing would bring enemy reinforcements before he could shell the main Choiseul Bay base. As an alternative target he had been assigned the enemy installations on Guppy Island, which was closer. Under the circumstances he decided to direct his fire there. With the trees growing out over the beach, he had to place his 60-millimeter mortars in the water, their muzzles protruding only a few inches above the surface. When he gave the order a hundred and twenty rounds of high explosive shells soared into Guppy. As black smoke billowed from enemy fuel tanks and bewildered Japanese gunners on the island fired blindly in all directions, the Marines scooped up their mortars and hurried back to the Warrior, eager to board the LCPRs, which they expected to be waiting for them.

When they reached the river they were surprised to find that the LCPRs were not there. While they were waiting on the west bank for them to appear, several of the grimy Marines asked Bigger if they could clean off in the river. "Go ahead," he said. They had splashed only fifteen yards from shore when the stillness of the evening was ripped by Japanese machine guns and rifles firing from upstream on the same bank. This was the first that Bigger and his startled men knew that the enemy was on their flank. What they did not know—and what they had to find out quickly—was whether the Japanese were across the river also. If so, they were trapped with their backs to the sea and Japanese on three sides of them.

As PT 59 approached the Choiseul coast at sundown Kennedy was very much perturbed at seeing no sign of the boat that was to guide them to the Marines. Rhoads was sure that they had hit the island at approximately the spot indicated, but this did little to assuage Kennedy's sense of frustration. Knowing that men in trouble somewhere were depending on them, he said that they had to try to find the boat. Perhaps they were too far down the coast.

Turning north, he kicked up his engines to a degree that made Drawdy wince in front of the gasoline gauge. Half their supply was gone already. After a fast run they approached an island with a red cliff that Kennedy and Rhoads recognized as Moli. This meant that they had gone too far north. Kennedy wheeled south again, and as he was returning to the area whence they had come, he saw a landing craft three hundred yards off the shore. As he approached he recognized to his surprise a fellow PT skipper, Lt. (jg) Richard E. Keresey, standing on the gunwale looking as though he were ready to leap across fifty feet of sea to get into PT 59. The landing craft had been damaged and was delayed by repairs in getting on station to meet them.

"Dick, what are you doing over there?" Kennedy asked as he pulled alongside and Keresey jumped aboard.

"Never mind that now," Keresey said. "We've got to get up the line in a hurry. Some Marines are in real trouble."

Kennedy and Keresey had met in Tulagi Harbor in the spring when Kennedy gave Keresey a tow to drydock after Keresey's boat had been damaged on a reef. During the summer they were at Rendova together. Keresey piloted PT 105 in Blackett Strait the night PT 109 was sunk. Speeding toward the Warrior River, he told Kennedy that he had been sent in with the Marines to reconnoiter the coast for a PT base in case it was decided to operate boats out of Choiseul. He gave Kennedy as much information as he had on Bigger's predicament. LCPRs would go in to pick up the patrol, he explained, but the fire power of the PTs would be needed to hold the Japanese back from the shore and give the Marines a chance to embark. Kennedy ordered his gunners to stand ready to cover the evacuation.

A few miles north of PT 59 the Japanese were closing in on the Marines, and Bigger's situation was desperate. He supposed that Duncan's squad was still on the east bank and sent an officer and two men across the river to make contact with them. Duncan and his men had left hours earlier for help. Indeed, having rounded up the LCPRs at Nukiki, they were now approaching the Warrior River a couple of miles ahead of Kennedy in PT 59. The three men crossing the river were fired on from the east bank. Two were killed. Bigger now knew that he was completely surrounded.

As darkness fell a fresh exchange of fire swept through the jungle. Corporal Edward James Schnell, of Wilmette, Illinois, fell critically wounded with a bullet through his right chest. Lt. Stevens, the medical officer, and a pharmacist's mate carried him to the shore.

"Doc, don't leave me," Schnell pleaded.

"I'm not going to leave you, Jimmy," Stevens said.

To the surprise of the Japanese and the joy of the Marines two LCPRs appeared out of the darkness. The enemy gunners turned their fire on the boats as they approached the shore. The ensign who was the coxswain of the leading boat shouted that it was impossible to land against such fire and was turning back when Marine Sergeant Rahland Wilson drew his .45, pointed it at the ensign and said, "Go in."

Under the cover of fire from the Marines in the two boats Bigger's men waded out over the coral flat. Several of them carried Schnell through the water. When the first boat was loaded, she left for Voza. Schnell was lifted into the crowded second boat, and after Bigger, Stevens and the rest had scrambled in, the boat started out. The firing from the shore had ceased in the darkness. To the exhausted Marines, the rescue coming at the very moment of disaster seemed miraculous.

The sea had been rising during the early evening. As the second boat was leaving she sprang a leak from pounding on the coral. At first the accident seemed trivial. The boat pulled away from shore without difficulty, and the Marines relaxed with the sweet feeling of being alive. As the boat moved out through the opening in the reef, however, water began flooding the engine housing.

Only gradually did it dawn on those aboard that their feelings of relief and security were a complete illusion. Under the weight of the load and the hammering of the waves the leaking boat was sinking. Fear gripped the men. In the rising water the engine stalled. The frenzied efforts of the crew could not get even a cough out of it. The other LCPR had vanished in the night. The exultation of escape was snuffed out by the terrible realization that the waves were delivering the Marines back to the Japanese waiting on the shore.

At the height of despair a voice among the Marines shouted almost hysterically, "Here's a PT boat!"

The terrified men looked through the night and saw PT 59 coming toward them through the waves. They could hear the welcome sound of throbbing engines and splashing exhaust. By now they were so low in the water that the motor torpedo boat loomed unnaturally large and formidable. Her two 40-millimeter guns pointed to the dark sky, and the rows of machine guns along her sides where the torpedo tubes used to be were trained on the shore. Helmeted men scurried about the deck making ready to come alongside the sinking boat.

Idling his engines, Kennedy steered between the foundering LCPR and the shore. The Japanese might concentrate heavy fire on him at any moment. He dared not think what a perfect target PT 59 would be a few hundred yards off shore if but a single flare should burst above them now.

When he edged the boat against the LCPR, the PT crew began hauling aboard the soaked Marines who were almost incoherent with gratitude. Stevens asked for help to lift Schnell onto PT 59.

"Lieutenant," Stevens told Kennedy, "I've got a man in bad shape here."

"We'll find a place for him," Kennedy said.

Some forty to fifty Marines were spilling over into every foot of space on the boat. The deck swarmed with them. They were perched on the day-room canopy, crowded onto the fantail, jammed into the crew's quarters. There was scarcely room for the PT sailors to move about in.

"Any left?" Kennedy called back from the cockpit. In addition to the threat of fire from the shore, he and Rhoads were worried that the Japanese might come out in barges to attack them.

"Major Bigger," a Marine called, "this here officer"—pointing to Kennedy— "wants to know if everybody is aboard."

"It's okay to go," Bigger said.[†]

Every man aboard was aching to get out of range of the Japanese guns. Kennedy pushed his throttles forward, and PT 59, severely overloaded, responded sluggishly. The problem of weight alarmed him. PT 59 was getting rather old and shaky, in any case. The armor taxed its hull. Now, with anywhere from fifty-five to sixty-five men aboard, he had visions of the boat's falling apart in the waves.

A path through the swarming passengers was cleared for Schnell, and the wounded corporal was carried down into the skipper's quarters below the cockpit and laid in Kennedy's bunk. On deck a Marine suddenly became hysterical, and Bigger strove patiently to calm him. Kennedy had seen many of these Marines before they embarked from Vella Lavella on October 27 and thought they were the fittest-looking troops he had ever encountered. Beholding them in their present condition, he was surprised to see how thoroughly men could be transformed in one week. Mauer gave the hungry Marines such food as he could scrape together in the galley. In the engine room Drawdy watched with resignation as the gasoline ran slowly out and the engines overheated from the load.

When they were underway to Voza, where PT 59 had been ordered to bring the rescued Marines, Kennedy dropped down

---

[†]When in the preparation of this book calls were made to Colonel Bigger and Dr. Stevens to solicit their recollection of these events, neither man had the slightest idea of the identity of the PT skipper who had rescued them in the dark off Choiseul. When they were told it was President Kennedy they were incredulous. "You're pulling my leg," Dr. Stevens reprimanded me.

to his quarters and asked Stevens if anything could be done to assist him in the treatment of Schnell. Stevens said that he would rig up a plasma bottle and sew Schnell's wounds as best he could with the few instruments he had.

"Am I all right, doc?" Schnell asked.

"Jimmy, don't worry about it," Stevens said. "You're going to be all right."

In a letter recommending young Schnell to the Marine Corps, the postmaster of Wilmette, where Schnell attended high school, wrote that he had seen Schnell "grow from a little boy into a young man" and predicted, "Edward will serve his country well and with honor."

At Voza the Marines were transferred into landing craft. Schnell's condition was so critical that he could not be moved and it was decided that Stevens should remain with him aboard PT 59 on the trip back to Vella Lavella. It was after midnight when Kennedy started across the Slot. From time to time he went down to his bare, dim quarters to see if Stevens needed help. The doctor had sewed the wounds in his patient's back and chest and was holding his hand. Looking into the fading light in the young Marine's eyes one knew there was no hope, At sea at 1 A.M. on November 3 Corporal Schnell died quietly in Kennedy's bunk.

Kennedy was not in the room at the time. Stevens climbed wearily up to the cockpit and told him. Kennedy shook his head, but did not say anything. At 3 A.M. the engines went dead as the last drop of gasoline was consumed. The other PT boat threw a line over and towed PT 59 back to Lambu Lambu Cove.

KENNEDY'S DAYS OF COMBAT were about over. The trauma and strain of the collision in Blackett Strait and the many hours of swimming that followed it were beginning to tell. His back pained him, and he had spells of feeling poorly. The disc between his fifth vertebra and his sacrum was ruptured. The abnormal strains of the crash and the swimming had done certain lasting damage to his adrenal glands. Furthermore he had contracted malaria, possibly during the time when he was castaway without atabrine. He consulted a Navy doctor on Vella Lavella, but continued as skipper of PT 59 while the doctor considered his case.

The night after the rescue of Bigger's men PT 59 and four other boats returned to Choiseul to escort three landing craft taking out more Marines now that the mission of the 2nd Marine Battalion had been completed. On the night of November 8–9 Kennedy and three other boats prowled off Choiseul Bay looking for barges. On the night of November 11–12 while on the way from Moli Island to Choiseul Bay, Kennedy chased two barges emerging from the Emerald Entrance but the barges turned back into the harbor and safety.

On the night of November 13–14 Kennedy was sent back to the Choiseul Bay area again and shelled Sipasa and Guppy Islands. A plane came up on PT 59's stern at 4:35 A.M. during their return to Lambu Lambu. The gunners opened fire, and the plane disappeared.

To the end the Japanese privy over the water beckoned the gunners. As Kennedy was returning from one of his final patrols he passed the island where it was situated and, as usual, was implored to take the proper military action against it. Somehow his earlier objections did not seem so compelling now. On the radio he obtained permission for a bit of target practice. "Fire!" the command was given. The last remnants of Hirohito's empire on that beach went up in smoke and splinters.

On the fourteenth, Kennedy wrote a letter of comic congratulations to his brother Robert, on hearing the news that Robert, at seventeen, had been inducted into the Navy.

Robert F. Kennedy
The Milton School
Milton, Conn.

Nov. 14

Dear Robert:

The folks sent me a clipping of you taking the oath. The
sight of you up there, just as a boy, was really moving particularly as a close examination showed that you had my
checked London coat on. I'd like to know what the hell
I'm doing out here while you go stroking around in my
drape coat, but I suppose that what we are out here for,
or so they tell us, is so that our sisters and younger brothers will be safe and secure—frankly, I don't see it quite that
way—at least, if you're going to be safe and secure, that's
fine with me, but not in my coat, brother, not in my coat.
In that picture you looked as if you were going to step
outside the room, grab your gun, and knock off several of
the house-boys before lunch. After reading Dad's letter,
I gathered that cold vicious look in your eye was due to
the thought of that big blocking back from Groton. I
understand that you are going to be there till Feb. 1, which
is very nice because it is on the playing fields of Milton
and Groton, and maybe Choate, that the seeds will be
sown that in later years, and on other fields, will cause
you to turn in to sick bay with a bad back or a football
knee.

Well, black Robert, give those Grotties hell and keep in
contact with your old broken down brother. I just took the
physical examination for promotion to full Looie. I
coughed hollowly, rolled my eyes, croaked a couple of
times, but all to no avail. Out here, if you can breathe,
you're one A. and "good for active duty anywhere," and

by anywhere, they don't mean El Morocco or the Bath and Tennis Club, they mean right where you are. See you soon, I hope.

Jack

Kennedy's final action in World War II was on the night of November 16–17 when he took PT 59 across the Slot on an uneventful patrol to see what might be going on around Redman Island. On November 18 the log of PT 59 contained this entry:

Moored at base. 0800 Mustered—no absentees. 0900— Took aboard 700 gals. fuel. Arrived at Buloa.† Lt. J. Kennedy left boat as directed by Dr. at Lambu Lambu. (Ensign J. Mitchell took over as Capt. of PT 59)

When PT 59 docked at Biloa, Kennedy, looking thin and tired, walked quietly along the deck shaking hands with his men. He had a particularly hard time bringing himself to say good-by to the members of the old crew of PT 109 who were still with him—Maguire, Kowal, Drawdy, Drewitch and Mauer. "If there is ever anything I can do for you, ask me," he said. "You will always know where you can get in touch with me." As the years went by, knowing where they could get in touch with him was to become easier and easier for the crew.

With that he turned PT 59 over to Ensign Mitchell and walked down the path that led to the airstrip.

On his way home Kennedy spent a couple of days with friends in Beverly Hills and called Mrs. McMahon, who was living in Los Angeles. He wanted to see her but did not feel up to going into the city. Instead she went out to spend the afternoon with him and thought he looked pale and weak. He told her the story of the collision in Blackett Strait and gave her a full

---

†Biloa, in the southern part of Vella Lavella, where the Allies had an airstrip.

account of Pat's ordeal on Plum Pudding and Olasana. He assured her, however, that when he had bade him good-by at Tulagi her husband was coming along very well. In time McMahon recovered completely from his burns.

In Miami, where he was assigned briefly as an instructor in a PT training program, Kennedy pecked out a letter on a typewriter to Maguire:[†]

"Went up before the Survey Board the other day—an I'm on the way out. It's going to seem peciliar paying full prices at those movie theaters again. It won't seem quite right until everyone is out, I don't think. Going to spend Christmas with the folks. . . ."

Kennedy telephoned the Kirksey family in Georgia to express his condolences. He had Johnston, who was now back at Melville, go on his behalf to the Marneys in Springfield. In the spring of 1944, after his weight had dropped to 125 pounds, he entered the New England Baptist Hospital in Boston for the first of two disc operations. One of his early visitors was Johnston, who, in his bluff manner, barged into the room, saying, "Hey, have they converted you?" The Marneys also were visitors.

While he was recuperating that summer many of his South Pacific buddies were back at Melville. In August he had Thom, Ross, Fay and Reed down to Hyannis Port for a merry weekend. "Honey Fitz," who was to live until 1950, was on hand and charmed them with a couple of Irish jigs and a story or two that his wife scolded him for telling.

Later on, Kennedy, Johnston, Maguire and McMahon participated in a war-bond program in Boston and then, along with Mrs. McMahon and Mrs. Johnston, spent the weekend at Hyannis Port. Gasoline rationing was still a problem. McMahon, his South Pacific training standing him in good stead, scrounged

---

[†]Spelling his.

enough gas off a PT boat in Melville to get him to Hyannis Port in his 1936 Ford. Luckily the Kennedys had enough on hand to get him back. In 1946 Kennedy invited Maguire, whose home is Jacksonville Beach, to come to Boston for a convention of the Veterans of Foreign Wars, at which Kennedy, now just entering politics, was one of the principal speakers. That fall Fay came east from California to help him in his winning campaign for the House of Representatives.

After this a number of years passed during which Kennedy saw little of his crew, who were scattered across the land. From their homes, however, the men watched with great interest as Kennedy, after serving three terms in the House, was elected to the Senate and then, in 1956, was nearly nominated for Vice-President at the Democratic National Convention in Chicago, where Senator Estes Kefauver edged him out in a thrilling roll call.

The years of separation of skipper and crew came to an end in 1960 when Kennedy ran for the Presidency. Johnston and Ross, after receiving a call from Fay, joined Kennedy in Milwaukee for a program that was part of his campaign in the Wisconsin primary. After Kennedy won the nomination at Los Angeles several of the crew worked hard for his election. Ross became Chairman of Citizens for Kennedy in Barrington, Illinois. Maguire got a merchant to donate a store and opened a Citizens for Kennedy office in Jacksonville Beach, which Kennedy carried by more than 100 votes. Drewitch was chairman of Citizens for Kennedy in Champagne County, Illinois, and, in addition, made speeches all over the state. In Cathedral City, California, Pat McMahon, now a mail carrier, sat idly by in frustration because the Hatch act forbade him, as a federal employee, from taking part in the campaign.

The great reunion came on January 20, 1961, when the crew of PT 109 gathered in Washington to see John F. Kennedy inaugurated as the thirty-fifth President of the United States. He had arranged a meeting with them the night before, but the jinx of 109 had one breath left. The worst snowstorm that Washington had seen in decades strangled traffic, and Kennedy could not get to the reception.

One of his first Presidential acts, however, was to give a hearty wave and big grin to the crew as they passed on a float in the inaugural parade aboard a PT boat numbered 109 in memory of the old hulk on the bottom of Blackett Strait. President Kennedy's experiences on that boat and the pain that resulted had made him a wiser, stronger and more confident man. It is even possible that he might never have reached the White House if it had not been for PT 109.

AFTERWORD
TO THE 40TH ANNIVERSARY EDITION

DUANE HOVE

FORTY YEARS after its first publication, Robert Donovan's *PT 109* remains a fresh and highly readable account of John F. Kennedy's wartime experiences. It is a credit to Donovan's skills as a journalist and author that he researched and wrote this book within nine months after McGraw-Hill commissioned him to do so.

The purpose of this afterword is to provide new background and context for Donovan's original narrative, including points about the story that have remained controversial, and a thorough look at PT boats, from concept to construction and training to actual service.

We begin by reexamining Kennedy's role in the evacuation of the Marine patrol at Warrior River at Choiseul Island. Here was a mission with all the dangers and all the daring of the PT 109 incident in Blackett Strait. Because it was not the story Donovan was charged to write, however, Donovan devoted only ten pages to it.

PT 59 AT WARRIOR RIVER

After having spent about three weeks recuperating from his survival odyssey in Blackett Strait, Kennedy was given command of a second boat, PT 59, by Squadron 2 Commanding Officer Alvin Cluster. Kennedy oversaw PT 59's conversion from a torpedo boat to a gunboat: the four torpedo tubes and the 20 mm Oerlikon cannon were removed and replaced by a 40 mm Bofors cannon and six .50-caliber machine guns. Work was begun at the Tulagi Island PT boat base. A repair ship anchored in Purvis Bay on Florida Island performed the heavy conversion work.

Kennedy took PT 59 up to the PT boat base at Lambu Lambu Cove on the northeast coast of Vella Lavella Island in mid-October 1943. Lieutenant LeRoy Taylor had established this remote base a few weeks earlier with a handful of PT boats from Squadron 11, a small support ship, and little else. The PT boats conducted patrols off nearby Choiseul Island to interdict Japanese barge traffic. Ten days after PT 59 arrived at Vella Lavella, Lieutenant Colonel Victor Krulak led 750 Marines from the 2nd Marine Parachute Battalion ashore on the west coast of Choiseul near the village of Voza. Their mission was to draw the Japanese military's attention away from the impending Allied invasion of Bougainville Island at Empress Augustus Bay. Krulak would soon meet the young PT 59 boat captain and remain in touch with him as a Marine Corps general during Kennedy's White House years.

On the evening of November 2, 1943, PT 59 assisted in the evacuation of one of Krulak's patrols, largely composed of Marines from Company G, which was boxed in by Japanese soldiers. The 87-man Marine patrol, led by Battalion Executive Officer Major Warner Bigger, had shelled Japanese installations on the north end of Choiseul and then maneuvered back to their rendezvous point at the mouth of the Warrior River. The Marines encountered heavy Japanese resistance as they reached the river's northeast bank. Learning that Japanese soldiers had isolated the patrol, Krulak radioed Marine Headquarters on Guadalcanal for assistance. Headquarters sent an urgent message to the PT boat base at Lambu Lambu Cove requesting immediate support. Only PT 59 and PT 236 were available, and Kennedy's PT 59 had just 700 gallons of fuel onboard. The two boats left immediately to aid the Marines, aware that PT 59 would run out of fuel on the return trip.

Upon arrival at Voza near dusk, the two PT boat crews met PT boat captain Dick Keresey, who had accompanied the Marine invasion force in order to scout for a possible PT boat base. Keresey came aboard PT 59 and guided the PT boats up to the Marines' location at Warrior River. Three personnel landing craft from Voza, with a Marine squad onboard, had preceded the PT boats, engaged the enemy with machine gun fire, and embarked the Marines under cover of a rain squall. As they departed the shore, however, one of the landing craft was damaged by a coral reef when negotiating the heavy surf. A second landing craft attempted to tow the disabled landing craft but was having great difficulty due to the excess weight and high seas. Although the enemy fire had diminished in the presence of the counter fire and the rain squall, the disabled landing craft was in danger of foundering. Then, in what must have appeared to the Marines to be a miracle, two PT boats emerged from the darkness. The PT boats offloaded the Marines from the three landing craft and escorted the two serviceable landing craft back to the Marine base at Voza. After debarking the Marines via landing craft, the two PT boats headed back to Lambu Lambu Cove with several wounded Marines and Keresey aboard. As expected, PT 59 ran out of fuel around 3:00 A.M. and had to be towed the rest of the way.

When Kennedy's service in the Pacific is remembered, it is most often in the context of the sinking of PT 109 in Blackett Strait and the subsequent rescue of the shipwrecked crew. The incident at Warrior River, however, is far more representative of the use of PT boats and their brave crews. Dick Keresey's book *PT 105* gives a full account of this.

PT BOAT DEVELOPMENT

U.S. Patrol Torpedo boats used in World War II had their origin in World War I–vintage European Motor Torpedo Boats. After

World War I, the U.S. Navy attempted to duplicate with PT boats the achievements of the British, German, and Italian navies by developing its own Motor Torpedo Boats subsequently designated PT boats. But initial PT boat development efforts in the United States were unsatisfactory. Then, in what proved to be an insightful move, the Electric Boat Company's Elco Division obtained a license to produce the British Hubert Scott-Paine design instead of undertaking costly reengineering. Elco built ten of the 70-foot Scott-Paine boats in its Bayonne, New Jersey, plant in early 1940. These boats were subsequently loaned to the British as part of the Lend Lease program.

Under Navy direction, Elco lengthened the Scott-Paine boat to 77 feet, primarily to be able to carry the Mark VIII 21-inch torpedo. The 77-foot Elco, a 78-foot boat entered by Higgins Industries, Inc., of New Orleans, Louisiana, and a 78-foot boat entered by the Huckins Yacht Corporation of Jacksonville, Florida, were selected through a Navy design competition for an expanded construction program.

When the Navy subsequently issued specifications for a larger PT boat, which led to an 80-foot Elco redesign, Higgins and Huckins stuck with their 78-foot designs. The Navy issued initial contracts to all three companies, though the Navy's first eight-boat order with Huckins turned out to be the last because of the boats' poor performance. Higgins, better known for producing landing craft, would eventually build 199 PT boats, but Elco was the big winner, producing 326 80-foot PT boats during the war. A handful of PT boats were also built by Canadian Power Boat, Harbor Boat Building, R. Jacob, the Annapolis Yacht Yard, and the Herreshoff Yard in Bristol, Rhode Island.

In December 1941, the Navy was woefully short of warships needed to fight the newly declared two-ocean war. A massive shipbuilding program was underway, but it would be at least a year before a substantial number of warships could be turned out. Thus, PT boats filled the immediate need of getting firepower into battle. It was not coincidental that the PT boats were built of wood and therefore would not tie up steel ship construction yards. The Navy's original role for the PT boats was to deliver fast torpedo attacks. As the war progressed, PT boats were used in an increasing range of missions, from barge busting to rescuing downed pilots.

PT BOAT CONSTRUCTION AND OUTFITTING

PT boats were manufactured of wood in a rapid but labor-intensive process. Prefabricated bulkheads of spruce, white oak, and mahogany were assembled inverted in a jig. Marine plywood was placed over the bulkheads and sealed. The keel and the chines were then secured to the structure with brass bolts. Two layers of mahogany planks were laid up crosswise to each other over the plywood, with aircraft fabric soaked in marine glue between the layers for added strength. The hull was turned over and deck planks were added. Machinery, tankage, superstructures, galley equipment, sleeping accommodations, fittings, and weapons were installed. Early Elco 77-foot boats weighed 33 tons, the Elco 80-foot boats 38 tons, and the Higgins 78-foot boats 43 tons.

PT boats were powered by three 1,200 hp Packard engines that burned 100-octane aviation gasoline. Over the course of the war, engine refinements improved their power to 1,500 hp. The PT boats had a top speed of 40 to 45 knots, depending on load and sea state, though 55 knots was once recorded on a glassy sea off Melville, Rhode Island. A typical cruising speed was about 30 knots, and a typical patrol speed was 8 to 10 knots. The three Packard engines consumed 300 (cruising) to 500 (full throttle) gallons of fuel per hour. For very long voyages, extra fuel was transported in barrels on deck or in a tender that accompanied the boats.

PT boats were initially armed with four Mark VIII torpedoes

carried in steel tubes on deck. When the boats were underway at high speed, the tubes were sealed with a dome cover to keep out ocean spray and were aligned with the boat's keel to avoid being struck by waves. Before the torpedoes could be fired, the crew had to remove the dome covers and manually angle the tubes outward so the torpedoes would clear the deck. Black powder charges expelled the torpedoes forward from the tubes. To fire a charge, the captain, executive officer, or quartermaster pushed a button in the cockpit, sending an electrical impulse to the igniter. If the charges failed to ignite, the torpedo man would strike a percussion cap with a wooden mallet. Later in the war, the Mark VIII torpedoes and their tubes were replaced by the lighter Mark XIII torpedo mounted on roll-out racks.

Armament included two twin .50-caliber turret guns amid-ships, as well as a 20 mm Oerlikon cannon and two 300-pound depth charges. Mortars, machine guns, and rockets were some-times substituted for standard armament.

Smoke generators mounted on the aft deck were used to lay down a smoke screen to aid in escape. Early PT boats had no radar; this crucially important equipment was retrofitted to the early boats starting in mid-1943. It is quite possible that if PT 109 had been one of the boats retrofitted, it would have been able to avoid being rammed.

PT BOAT MEN

Hundreds of new boats required hundreds of new crews. A typ-ical PT boat crew size was two officers and ten enlisted men; however, crews were replaced after a year in combat. Men were also needed for base construction and operation, communica-tions, intelligence, equipment repair, clerical duties, and supply as well as for PT boat tenders.

The Navy's primary training facility was the Motor Torpedo Boat Squadrons Training Center at Melville, Rhode Island.

Classroom instruction was coupled with seagoing training on Melville's Squadron 4 PT boats. Approximately 2,500 officers and 20,000 enlisted men were trained at Melville. Not everyone went through the training center, however. It has been estimated that more than 50,000 men served in PT boats, their base forces, or their tenders.

Crews were assigned to newly delivered boats and sent on shakedown trials. Elco boats and crews initially underwent shakedown at Melville, while Higgins boats were shaken down at a facility adjoining the Submarine Chaser Training Center in Miami, Florida. After 1943, all shakedown trials were conducted in Florida.

The Navy began recruiting men for Melville by sending veteran PT boat officers to speak at Navy training schools. Young men rushed to apply. And why not? The speakers described exciting battle experiences while operating from cobbled-together bases in the Philippine and Solomon Islands. Daily life for PT boat crews was not as regimented as aboard a ship of the line. Dress codes and saluting were nonexistent. Young officers were captains of their own ships and enjoyed a reputation for being dashing and independent. Their role was glamorized in newspaper accounts and the 1942 best-selling book *They Were Expendable*. As PT boat production was gearing up in 1943, *LIFE* magazine and the book *Long Were the Nights* dramatically described PT Squadron 3(2)'s battles against Japanese cruisers and destroyers off Guadalcanal. Navy recruiters no doubt appreciated the publicity.

Having held two desk jobs, Ensign Kennedy requested sea duty and in the summer of 1942 was ordered to the Naval Reserve Midshipmen's School at Northwestern University. He had been directly commissioned an Ensign so had no formal Navy training. Kennedy took an accelerated course designed to produce seagoing officers in sixty days. He was at Northwestern when Lieutenant Commander John Bulkeley and Lieutenant John Harllee came to recruit officers for Melville. An experienced small-boat seaman, young Kennedy applied for this well-publicized branch of the Navy. When he completed his Midshipman training in September, he was ordered to Melville for an eight-week course in PT boat operation. After Kennedy's December graduation, Harllee assigned him to duty as a Melville instructor, but Kennedy requested combat duty, instead. He was sent to the South Pacific as a replacement officer, arriving on Tulagi Island in mid-April 1943.

PT BOAT SERVICE AREAS

Early PT boat squadrons were based in Hawaii and the Philippines. Indeed, the crews of PT boat Squadron 1 were among the first to fire back at Japanese aircraft attacking Pearl Harbor. In March 1942, four PT boats from Squadron 3, led by Lieutenant John Bulkeley, evacuated General Douglas MacArthur and his party from Corregidor. Bulkeley was awarded the Congressional Medal of Honor for this daring voyage through Japanese-controlled waters. Several month later, Squadron 1 boats helped defend Midway Island during attack by Japanese carrier aircraft.

PT boats were sent to Palmyra and Funafuti to help protect these vital way stations for aircraft and ships bound for the South Pacific. Kennedy's Squadron 2 commanding officer Alvin Cluster was stationed at Funafuti when he participated in the rescue of World War I flying ace Eddie Rickenbacker, whose aircraft had crashed on a visit to the South Pacific. Other early PT boats went to the Aleutian Islands and the Solomon Islands. As the battle front moved up the Solomons and the north coast of New Guinea, PT boats moved with it. American PT boats participated in the invasions of North Africa and Sicily, the Italian campaign, the Normandy invasion, and the invasion of southern France. When Japanese Naval forces attempted to dislodge General

MacArthur's invasion forces at Leyte Beach, PT boats were the first to counter their cruisers and destroyers in Surigao Strait.

Although PT boats and crews performed admirably in all theaters, their performance in the Solomon Islands campaign had a significant impact on operations there. PT boats were sent to Tulagi in October 1942 to harass Japanese cruisers and destroyers that were shelling U.S. Marines on Guadalcanal at night. The PT boats did more than "harass," however: a handful of Squadron 3(2) PT boats attacked and sank several Japanese destroyers and a Japanese submarine. Japanese destroyers were later called upon to protect supply convoys from this new menace. U.S. Naval forces responded with more PT boats and a well-timed battleship and destroyer attack commanded by Admiral Willis "Ching" Lee. In the face of a constant threat, the Japanese convoys elected to dump supplies overboard and let them drift into shore.

With the Japanese abandonment of Guadalcanal, large ships became too valuable for Japan to risk in the close quarters of the Solomon Islands and the inlets and bays on the north coast of New Guinea. Barges operating at night close to shore took over supplying remote bases. PT boats, with their speed, agility, and shallow draft, were ideal for intercepting and attacking the barges. Japan upped the ante by armoring the barges and assigning troops with small arms to them. The PT boats countered by adding 37 and 40 mm cannon. Frustrated by the slowdown in shipping, Japan called upon four destroyers to resupply the important Japanese base at Vila on Kolombangara Island to support the defense of Munda on New Georgia Island. They succeeded on the night of August 1–2 despite the efforts of fifteen PT boats in Blackett Strait. On the night of August 6–7, however, three of the four Japanese destroyers were sunk by U.S. destroyers in the battle of Vella Gulf. That action put an end to Japan's use of destroyers to resupply remote bases, and Japan returned to using barges for resupply.

OPERATIONAL DIFFICULTIES

The wooden-hulled PT boats, carrying 3,000 gallons of aviation fuel, were highly vulnerable to enemy attack. A well-placed bomb or naval shell could disintegrate a PT boat. Consequently, the PT boats almost always operated at night.

Nocturnal PT boats were detectable, however, by phosphorescent trails. Tiny animal and plant life in the warm South Pacific waters would literally glow when excited by the PT boat's wake turbulence. Japanese aircraft, particularly float planes flying low and slow, would simply follow the glowing trail and bomb or strafe the tip of the trail. When transiting to patrol areas, PT boat skippers were forced to keep their speed down to minimize their wake's turbulence.

Operating at night led to other problems. Firing torpedoes would sometimes ignite the torpedo tube's sealing grease and lubricating oil, thereby highlighting the PT boat. Night operation also contributed to frequent running aground on poorly charted shoals and reefs. Poor visibility led to improper identification that resulted in attacks by friendly forces—and vice versa. Finally, it was not uncommon to lose sight of companion PT boats and fall out of formation. This is precisely what happened to PT 109 in Blackett Strait.

Another difficulty was the constant maintenance required by the Packard engines. Often operating from remote bases without adequate repair facilities, the engines on PT boats failed repeatedly. As the war progressed, many engines far exceeded their 600-hour lifetimes but were patched up and returned to service because of severe replacement shortages.

Torpedoes were a problem, as well. The World War I–vintage Mark VIII torpedoes were largely ineffective. In fact, when reports of torpedo failures in the South Pacific reached Washington, Naval laboratory tests were conducted that revealed that over half of the torpedo warheads would not fire in controlled tests. Head-on encounters often caused the firing pin to fail and the warhead would not detonate. Torpedoes could not be used against shallow-draft barges, and one torpedo probably cost more than the barge itself.

CONTROVERSIES

With this fuller background on PT boats and their operation, we can now address the issues related to the sinking of PT 109 that made the incident controversial at the time—and that future revelations aren't likely to resolve completely.

Many critics find it impossible to believe that a nimble PT boat, operating in a war zone, could not get out of the way of an approaching enemy destroyer. PT 109 crewmen reported in interviews that, although the crew was at General Quarters, they simply could not get underway in the short time between the destroyer's sighting and the collision. PT 59 lookouts spotted the *Amagiri* only 10 to 20 seconds before the collision because of limited visibility on that overcast, moonless night. No PT boat remaining in Blackett Strait at the time had radar for an earlier detection, and no specific radio warning was received. Clearly, the practice of patrolling with only one engine engaged to keep the engine noise and wake turbulence down contributed greatly to the sinking of PT 109. When Kennedy signaled the engine room to engage the outer engines, the motor machinist had to manually shift the engines into gear. Then Kennedy had to bring the engines gradually up to speed to avoid stalling. All this takes time, certainly more than 10 or 20 seconds.

The evacuation of the Marines at Warrior River is not without controversy, as well. Various accounts have either two to three PT boats and either two to three landing craft present. This is easily settled: official records clearly show two PT boats and three landing craft. Depending on who is telling the story, differing versions range from PT boats going into the beach under intense fire with guns blazing to the PT boats unloading the landing craft well offshore under cover of a rain squall. One thing is certain, however: dozens of Marines owe their lives to the two brave PT boat crews.

There is some controversy about the appropriateness of Kennedy's medal award. He was not decorated for his seamanship or performance in battle: Kennedy, Thom, and Ross each received the Navy and Marine Corps Medal for their actions in effecting the rescue of the PT 109 crew. The medal is awarded for heroism not involving actual conflict with an enemy. For acts of lifesaving, it is required that the action be performed at the risk of one's own life. That seems appropriate.

Less a controversy than a misconception is Kennedy's medical discharge from the Naval Reserve. He was released from duty for chronic colitis, not for a back injury. Colitis was, in fact, the reason Kennedy was initially relieved from PT 59. The Naval Retiring Board concluded that the illness occurred after October 20, 1943, the date that Kennedy was promoted to lieutenant, undoubtedly because he had passed only a cursory physical exam in the Pacific. Kennedy went before the board in December 1944 and was placed on the retirement list on March 1, 1945.

POSTWAR

When World War II ended, the PT boats were disposed of and their crews sent back to the United States. A total of 720 PT boats were built, of which 531 were placed in U.S. Naval service. Britain and Russia were given the use of 188 PT boats under the Lend Lease program. Sixty-nine U.S. boats were lost in service, 26 by enemy action and 43 by accident or destruction to prevent enemy capture. After the war, the Navy had little use for the venerable PT boats, so only a few squadrons were kept at Melville for experimental purposes. Worn-out boats were stripped and burned—more than 100 off Samar alone. Serviceable boats were sold to entrepreneurs and sportsmen or were given to other nations, including Korea, China, and Yugoslavia.

Only a few PT boats survive today. Restored by PT Boats, Inc., PT 617 and PT 796 are on display at Battleship Cove in Fall River, Massachusetts. Currently, the Admiral Nimitz Foundation is restoring PT 309 for display at the Admiral Nimitz Museum and Historical Center in Fredericksburg, Texas. A handful of others exist in various configurations and states of repair.

Fifty-seven years after the sinking of PT 109, only one crewman who was onboard at the time, Gerard Zinser, is still alive. Men who served on PT 109 at other times are alive, among them Maurice Kowal, on medical leave from PT 109 the night she was sunk. Three PT 59 crew members who were on the Warrior River mission, Isaac Mitchell, Vivian Scribner, and Glen Christiansen, are living. Scores of PT boat men who served with Kennedy in the South Pacific are still living, but because there is no central organization that tracks PT boat servicemen, the total number of living PT veterans is unknown.

READERS WISHING to learn more about PT boats and their crews can do so by consulting these books:

At Close Quarters: PT Boats in the United States Navy, by Robert Johns Bulkley (Washington, D.C.: Naval History Division, U.S. Navy, 1962).

Knights of the Sea, by PT Boats, Inc. (Germantown, Tenn.: PT Boats, Inc., 1982).

Long Were the Nights: The Saga of PT Squadron "X" in the Solomons, by Hugh B. Cave (New York: Dodd, Mead, 1943).

They Were Expendable: An American Torpedo Boat Squadron in the U.S. Retreat from the Philippines, by W. L. White (Annapolis, Md.: Naval Institute Press, 1998).

United States PT-*Boats of World War II in Action,* by Frank D. Johnson (Poole, U.K.: Blandford Press, 1980).

Interested readers may also wish to join PT Boats, Inc., a nonprofit organization dedicated to the preservation of PT boat history (contact 901-755-8440 or www.ptboats.org/). Over 7,000 PT boat veterans are currently members of that organization.

Duane Hove
April 2001

PUBLISHER'S NOTE: Duane Hove's book *American Warriors: Five United States Presidents in the Pacific Theater* is forthcoming.

ABOUT THE AUTHOR

ROBERT J. DONOVAN's long and varied career as a journalist began in 1932. While writing *PT 109* in 1961, he was Chief of the Washington Bureau of the *New York Herald Tribune*, a position he later held for the *Los Angeles Times*. He is the author of numerous books, including *Eisenhower: The Inside Story*, a number-one bestseller in 1956; *The Assassins; Nemesis: Truman and Johnson in the Coils of War in Southeast Asia; Unsilent Revolution;* a two-volume history of the Truman presidency (*Conflict and Crisis* and *Tumultuous Years*); and *Boxing the Kangaroo: A Reporter's Memoir*. Donovan lives in Washington, D.C.